T0327712

Transformational Governance

How Boards Achieve Extraordinary Change

Beth Gazley and Katha Kissman

The Center for Association Leadership

WILEY

Published by John Wiley & Sons, Inc., Hoboken, New Jersey.
Published simultaneously in Canada.

For general information about our other products and services, please contact our Customer Care
Department within the United States at (800) 762-2974, outside the United States at (317) 572-3993 or
fax (317) 572-4002.

Wiley publishes in a variety of print and electronic formats and by print-on-demand. Some material
included with standard print versions of this book may not be included in e-books or in print-on-
demand. If this book refers to media such as a CD or DVD that is not included in the version you
purchased, you may download this material at http://booksupport.wiley.com. For more information
about Wiley products, visit www.wiley.com.

Library of Congress Cataloging-in-Publication Data:
Gazley, Beth, 1961–
    Transformational Governance: how boards achieve extraordinary change/Beth Gazley
and Katha Kissman.
        Pages cm
    Includes bibliographical references and index.
    ISBN 978-1-118-97672-2 (hardback); ISBN 978-1-118-97674-6 (ebk);
ISBN 978-1-118-97673-9 (ebk)
    1. Boards of directors.   2. Nonprofit organizations—Management.   3. Organizational change.
4. Corporate governance.   I. Kissman, Katha.   II. Title.
    HD2745.G39 2015
    658.4'22—dc23

                                                                        2015005241

Printed in the United States of America

10 9 8 7 6 5 4 3 2 1

Contents

Foreword

In my work with BoardSource, I often interact with individuals who are skeptical about the role that boards can play in advancing an organization's mission. Experiences with underperforming or dysfunctional boards have left them unconvinced about the positive value and potential for boards. They cite ineffective meetings, toxic interpersonal dynamics, and other all-too-common board frustrations; and they challenge the idea that investing in building an exceptional board is worth it, or even possible.

In our work, we aim to overcome this pessimism about the potential for boards and provide support to boards that are committed to strengthening their own impact. And each and every day we see boards that are making impressive and important leaps forward as they work to build their leadership potential and serve their missions better.

But the unfortunate fact remains that truly exceptional board leadership is not the norm—a reality documented in BoardSource's report, *Leading with Intent: A National Index of Nonprofit Board Practices 2015. Leading with Intent* found that, overall, boards received a performance rating average of B minus. This underwhelming review of board performance helps explain the uphill battle that we face when challenging boards to aspire for truly exceptional leadership. More nonprofit leaders—board and staff alike—have experienced poor or mediocre board performance than have seen the transformational potential of a truly exceptional board.

That is why the stories of transformative change outlined in *Transformational Governance: How Boards Achieve Extraordinary Change* are so powerful. They are proof positive that investing the time and energy that it takes to build a strong and effective board is not only possible, but worth it. The organizations profiled are on the other side of that hard work and can point to stronger financial results, more engaged membership communities, and more satisfied executive leadership as a result of the investment that they have made in thoughtful and intentional board change.

Transformational Governance is not, however, about defining a desired outcome and mapping the path to get there. Instead, it is a study of the path itself.

It paints a picture of what the process of transformative change can look like for a nonprofit board. Carefully documented case studies are presented against a backdrop of quantitative research on high-performing association boards and useful frameworks for understanding change and human behavior.

It shares how boards have been able to move past "the way things have always been" to find a new way of leading their organizations into the future. And it offers practical guidance and first-person advice about how to identify, build the case for, and implement change at the board level.

The insights and practical guidance that *Transformational Governance* provides enable each nonprofit leader to gather their own observations and ideas for creating board change, and offer tangible suggestions about how to anticipate and overcome potential road blocks. Drawing heavily from established frameworks for leading change, the book connects readers with a broader community of change leaders, and builds confidence that positive, mission-focused, and results-oriented change is possible.

The heroes in the book are the board and staff leaders who share—with tremendous vulnerability and candor—what it took for their boards to transform themselves. As you read their stories, you are invited into the challenges, frustrations, and eventual successes of their change processes. They share what worked and what to watch out for, what they wish they had known and what they might have done differently. The experience of reading their stories leaves you with the feeling that you've received trusted counsel from a friend or colleague.

They also share why their investment in board change was worth it, how it positioned them to serve their missions and their members better, how it enabled them to embrace new opportunities or address longstanding issues, and in many cases, why they wish they had started their change process sooner.

As a result of their transformative changes, many of the nonprofit leaders profiled also reported a new orientation to change itself. Instead of viewing themselves as being at the end of a change process, they had embraced change as a way of being. They described a new culture of openness and dynamism, a commitment to flexible and adaptive leadership, and an awareness that truly exceptional board leadership means never being done growing and changing.

That is the challenge to each of us as readers. *Transformational Governance* is a hopeful and optimistic statement about the power of nonprofit board leadership. And it is a gentle but powerful call to action to nonprofit leaders. Strong board leadership is not only possible; it is worth the effort. And it's what our missions deserve.

Anne Wallestad
President and CEO
BoardSource

Acknowledgments

This book came about due to the vision and stewardship of the ASAE Foundation and John Wiley & Sons, Inc. In particular, the authors would like to thank Keith Skillman, CAE, vice president, publications, ASAE; Sharon Moss, PhD, CRA, CAE, chief research officer, and Chelsea Killam, director, research, both of the ASAE Foundation, along with the members of the ASAE Research Foundation Research Committee; and also Alison Hankey, former executive editor, Business Management, John Wiley & Sons, and Matthew Davis, senior editor, Wiley Business.

We also thank Bruce Lesley for referrals to interview subjects, and we thank those who read and endorsed the book and provided feedback on the study design and book drafts. We thank our colleagues at BoardSource and ARNOVA, as well as our many clients and students over the years, from all of whom we have learned so much. As always, we thank our families.

Most especially, we thank the more than 100 individuals who participated in this study, representing the associations listed here. Their insights into their experiences with board change created wonderfully inspirational stories, more than we had room for. Those stories are the core of this book and give it the impact and value we hope is offered to the nonprofit sector.

The associations are: Alabama Broadcasters Association, Alliance for Academic Internal Medicine, American Academy of Hospice and

Palliative Medicine, American Association of Pediatric Dentistry, American Board of Physician Specialties, American Camp Association, American Dental Association, American Dental Education Association, American Geophysical Union, American Health Information Management Association, American Network of Community Options and Resources, American Nurses Association, American Occupational Therapy Association, American School Counselors Association, American Society for Clinical Pharmacology and Therapeutics, American Society for Healthcare Risk Management, American Society for Parenteral and Enteral Nutrition, American Speech-Language-Hearing Association, APICS, Association for Corporate Growth, Association for Public Policy Analysis & Management, Association for Women in Science, Association of Legal Administrators, Association of Pool & Spa Professionals, California Association of Independent Schools, California Parks and Recreation Society, Competency & Credentialing Institute, Council of Colleges of Arts and Sciences, Cranberry Township Emergency Medical Services, Delta Sigma Phi, Delta Upsilon, Family Planning Advocates of New York State, Financial Services Institute, Home Building Association of Richmond, Indiana Bankers Association, Institute of Hazardous Materials Management, International Association of Lighting Designers, International Legal Technology Association, International Society for Technology in Education, International Society of Hair Restoration Surgery, Interstitial Cystitis Association, Iowa Association of Community College Trustees, Kansas Advocates for Better Care, Kappa Omicron Nu, League of Minnesota Cities, Manufacturers' Agents National Association, Metals Service Center Institute, Montana Credit Union Network, National Affordable Housing Management Association, National Alliance of Wound Care and Ostomy, National Architectural Accrediting Board, National Association for Catering and Events, National Association of Social Workers–Virginia Chapter, National Association of Trailer Manufacturers, National Communication Association, National Council for Community and Education Partnerships, National Council of University Research

Administrators, National Foundation for Credit Counseling, National Waste & Recycling Association, New England Nordic Ski Association, Northern Virginia Association of REALTORS®, Northwest Association of Independent Schools, Ohio AgriBusiness Association, Ohio Society of CPAs, Oregon Association of Hospitals and Health Systems, Pikes Peak Association of REALTORS®, Pinellas County Osteopathic Medical Society, Professional Ski Instructors of America and the American Association of Snowboard Instructors, Rubber Division–American Chemical Society, Society for Neuroscience, Society of Interventional Radiology, Society of Teachers of Family Medicine, Society of Tribologists and Lubrication Engineers, Society of Trust and Estate Practitioners, Solar Electric Power Association, Southeastern Museums Conference, Southern Association of Orthodontists, Southwest Association of Episcopal Schools, Southwestern Automated Clearing House Association, TESOL International Association, Texas Association of School Business Officials, Washington State Dental Association, Wisconsin Association of School Business Officials, Wisconsin Health Information Management Association, YMCA of Southern Nevada.

Introduction and Study Design

The highest levels of performance come to people who are centered, intuitive, creative, and reflective—people who know to see a problem as an opportunity.

—Deepak Chopra,
author, public speaker, and physician

The nonprofit sector is large and diverse, but on one point we agree: There has never been so much pressure on boards of directors to live up to stakeholders' expectations. A vast literature has accumulated on what good boards look like. Yet despite the accumulated knowledge, the burning question we hear often from nonprofit executives is, "We know what we are supposed to look like, but *how do we get there?*"

How do boards get from "good" to "great"? While many publications describe the qualities of nonprofit organizations that have already achieved high performance, this book uses real cases, compelling stories, and teachable moments to focus on the journey that organizations—specifically, member-serving nonprofit associations—took to get there. Ultimately, this book is designed to help boards move through a process beginning with identifying governance needs to self-education about better models and ultimately to successful self-improvement.

This book is intended for:

- Nonprofit executives, including presidents, CEOs, and executive directors; managing directors and chief operating officers; and other staff liaisons to boards.
- Trustees and directors, including chairs, officers, currently serving board members, and those considering board service.
- Owners of association management companies and their staff who work with nonprofit boards.
- Consultants and interim leaders working in the association management field.
- Scholars of good governance who are interested in evidence-driven research on strategic change management.
- Any other nonprofit managers, consultants, and advisors in search of a book on strategic change at the board level.
- Students in graduate programs and executive education courses on change management, association management, and board management. The emphasis in this book on case studies allows for a pedagogically appropriate application to the classroom setting to assess options, offer solutions, and then compare what actually happened with student recommendations. The cases could also be used in ongoing board development and education.

Why Another Book on Governance?

Excellent books already exist to help nonprofit leaders identify high-impact nonprofit practices. Now in a second edition, *Forces for Good* (Crutchfield and Grant 2012) has sold more than 50,000 copies. Jim Collins's *Good to Great* has been shared across all three sectors and spurred a follow-up monograph applicable to the social sectors. BoardSource has published *Exceptional Board Practices: The Source in Action* (2008) and *The Source: Twelve Principles of Governance That Power Exceptional Boards* (2005). Another joint publication of BoardSource and Jossey-Bass has also become a bestseller: *Governance as Leadership* (Chait, Ryan, and Taylor 2005). This literature joins plentiful resources from Jossey-Bass/Wiley, the Panel on the Nonprofit Sector, BoardSource, and elsewhere on the prescribed general duties and responsibilities of boards.

The association field has also produced several books on high-performing organizations and boards (some of which our interview subjects mentioned as instrumental in their board growth, in addition to those listed earlier). These include *7 Measures of Success* (ASAE and The Center for Association Leadership, 2006); *What Makes High Performing Boards* (ASAE; Gazley and Bowers 2013); *The Perfect Board, Third Edition* (Clemons 2011); *High-Impact Governing in a Nutshell* (ASAE; Eadie 2004), and *The Will to Govern Well* (ASAE; Tecker, Frankel, and Meyer 2002, now in a second edition, 2010).

Supporting this practitioner-oriented literature are dozens of scholarly books and articles on nonprofit governance. Recently, the Association for Research on Nonprofit Organizations and Voluntary Action (ARNOVA)—also a membership association, since it serves as the principal international learned society for nonprofit research—formed interest groups on board research and governance. There is scattered but growing interest in testing governance theories more broadly—see, for example, Will Brown's (2007) analysis of credit union board performance. The accumulating knowledge helped us frame this study by identifying the theories and variables that seem to matter most when explaining good governance.

Ultimately, we decided that while these valuable texts clearly have changed the nonprofit landscape for the better, an important gap in our common knowledge of good governance remains. This is addressed via three key contributions:

1. **A book that addresses the specific governance needs of member-serving organizations regardless of tax code.**

   Any discussion of good governance must begin with an understanding that a membership base changes the governance context. Associations may be organized around more complex chapter, section, or affiliate structures that complicate the board's ability to govern well. Associations are more likely to be led by member-elected boards and to place a stronger emphasis on representative or shared governance. Trade associations, in particular, may also rely on appointed board members. Bylaws may dictate bicameral governance structures or shared leadership responsibilities among several formal boards, which are known by many names ("councils of representatives," "houses of delegates," etc.). These features of the association world are not necessarily familiar to or regularly addressed in the general nonprofit board management literature.

Additionally, the existing research literature on good governance overemphasizes the context of 501(c)3 charities since historically these organizations have been subject to more public, media, regulatory, and scholarly scrutiny than nonprofits recognized under other parts of the tax code. But this situation will not continue forever given the pace of state and national regulatory activity. Indeed, all filing nonprofit organizations regardless of tax code have been meeting new governance expectations since a revised 990 informational return was introduced in 2008. Associations representing distinct and sometimes unique constituencies and micro-sectors (auctioneers, dog walkers, epidemiologists, automobile tire manufacturers, etc.) can just as easily get bogged down by past practices, misplaced assumptions of exceptionalism, and the baggage of organizational history as any other part of the nonprofit sector.

We suggest that studies of nonprofit performance that select their cases based on tax status may do a disservice to the sector. So this book is intended to help both (c)3 and non-(c)3 educational, research, social welfare, fraternal, and trade and professional associations meet public expectations. In other words, this book avoids false distinctions about what good governance means across tax codes, since good governance is expected of all nonprofit organizations. The focus instead is on the common experience of boards and the common need for public accountability regardless of mission.

In fact, 501(c)6 associations, on average, perform well when it comes to good governance, according to a recent analysis (Gazley 2014). Considerable attention has been focused on board development for trade and professional associations, and the importance of a strong board for both strategic and fiduciary reasons has been actively dis-

cussed for some time. So for those organizations, we offer an additional resource to help other (c)6 associations learn from their peers.

> *This book avoids false distinctions about what good governance means across tax codes since good governance is expected of all nonprofit organizations.*

2. A book that focuses on the change process itself.

An emphasis on the "journey" rather than the destination: This book focuses on elements missing or underemphasized in earlier practitioner publications. Many books have described the characteristics of high-performing nonprofit organizations. And there is also a small but growing interest in the role of nonprofit leadership in crisis management (see, for example, Reid and Turbide 2012). Absent, however, are resources and, at times, an understanding of the processes designed to guide nonprofit leaders through the stages of change that lead to higher perform-ance. But we know this kind of book is needed—BoardSource's 2012 Governance Survey (2013) found the majority of member organizations had completed a new strategic plan or launched a major initiative in the past two years. To support organizations dealing with change, this book emphasizes the journey to good governance and not simply the destination.

Diagnostic help: There is an emphasis on problem diagnosis and application of solutions by including the strategies, activities, and tools these associations used to achieve stronger governance. Many of the good governance books end with diagnostic tools, but few are aimed at helping organizations understand how to use the tools to identify problems and restructure themselves to perform better (there are exceptions, such as Tecker, Frankel, and Meyer's *The Will to Govern Well*). For example, we know that boards are advised to achieve a strategic orientation, but what has to change within an organization—and how do we change it—to become "strategic"? We use real stories of organizations that have walked the path of change to offer such guidance.

An unbiased approach to the tools: The *how-to* literature purchased often for board development tends to apply a particular framework or model developed by those authors at the possible expense of other valuable board-building strategies. By contrast, this book transcends specific models in favor of understanding the roles that any and all models play in improving association governance. As a result, among the stories and cases in this book, the reader will recognize popular governance tools but will also discover examples of associations that chose other strategies for improvement, or designed their own strategy.

3. **An evidence–driven book.**

This is principally a book for the practitioner, based in research. The cases, illustrations, and data on good governance practices included in this book emerged from three years of mixed methods research supervised by both a university institutional review board and a practitioner advisory committee (see the following Study Design section for details). The goal was to offer any CEO, board member, or consultant who is wrestling with the challenge of good governance evidence-driven information about how successful board change happens.

Our central theme of strategic change and change management is already of interest to nonprofit scholars. For example, governance experts have observed that research strategies treat boards too often as static entities. Scholars suggest that the nonprofit sector could benefit from more research into board dynamics, including how governance change happens (Cornforth 2012; Reid and Turbide 2012). Such a perspective supports a long-held view that all nonprofit performance is related in some way to board performance, so that board health is vital to the health of the nonprofit sector (Herman and Renz 1999).

Study Design

This book is based on two sources: ASAE's 2013 national survey of good governance practices, and new qualitative research produced for this book. The 2013 ASAE Governance Study, published in *What*

Makes High Performing Boards (Gazley and Bowers), used a stratified random sample, weighting, and other sophisticated techniques to produce a representative dataset of 1,585 association executives who were surveyed extensively on their board's structure, dynamics, and performance. The resulting analysis identified the key drivers of association board performance.

A key finding of the 2013 study, which became an important starting point for this second study, was the knowledge that most aspects of board *structure*, including board size, committee composition, meeting frequency, and recruitment practices, have less impact on performance than do board *dynamics*, specifically an association's success at forging strong board–staff relationships, creating a strategic orientation, and developing a culture of learning and accountability.

> *A key finding of the 2013 study was the knowledge that most aspects of board structure have less impact on performance than do board* dynamics.

This book therefore serves as somewhat of a sequel, to address a discussion point that emerged from the 2013 study: *Now that we understand what high-performing association boards look like, how do we help associations get there?* Study design began with discussions among governance experts and the ASAE Foundation's Research Advisory Committee (see Acknowledgments), feedback from conference presentations, an additional literature review, and a pilot focus group held during the ASAE annual meeting in Atlanta in August 2013. Portions of the study were conducted under the supervision of the Indiana University Institutional Review Board.

Because this is the first study (to our knowledge) that examines full-scale change management at the level of a nonprofit board of directors, we used structured interviews to capture the full story, followed by open coding of the interviews. In scholarly terms, this strategy produces qualitative case studies developed using the principles of grounded theory (Glaser and Strauss 2009). A grounded theory approach is recommended when the goal is new theory development or when it's uncertain how existing theories (particularly theories of change management) apply to the situations we are studying. The results include thematic organization of the cases throughout this book and presentation of the key concepts and ingredients of successful board change. We hope in turn that this material lends itself to future theory testing, now that we have captured the dynamics of governance change.

Data collection began by ranking participants in the 2013 study according to their assessment of their board's performance on 20 measures. The list of measures had been developed based on practitioner and academic literature reviews, cognitive interviews with association leaders, survey pretests, and consultation with governance experts (Gazley and Bowers 2013). Figures I.1 and I.2 display the performance measures and how the 1,585 association CEOs who participated in the 2013 survey ranked their boards. Overall, out of a total possible score of 60 (20 measures × top score of 3), the mean score was 38 and scores in the top quartile ranged from 44 to 60.

Based on each board's overall performance score, the CEOs representing approximately the top quartile ($N = 424$, 27 percent

"Considering the past two years, and in your own opinion, please rate the quality of board relations with various stakeholders, using the scale provided." ($N = 1,585$)

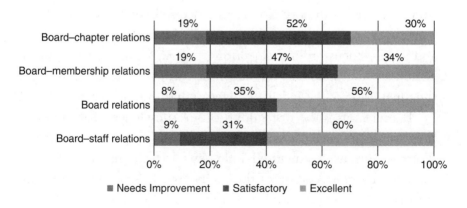

■ Needs Improvement   ■ Satisfactory   ■ Excellent

Figure I.1   CEO Assessments of Association Boards on Stakeholder Relations

Source: Gazley and Bowers (2013).

"Assessing the board as a whole, how would you rate the board's track record with respect to the following activities?" (*N* = 1,585)

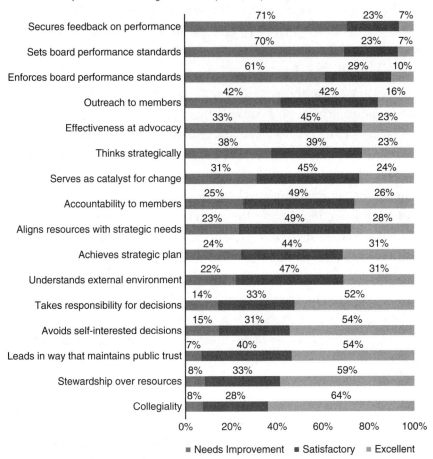

Figure I.2 CEO Assessments of Association Boards on Other Performance Measures

Source: Gazley and Bowers (2013).

of the sample) were contacted once by e-mail in March–April 2014, and asked to participate in a follow-up study if their high performance had involved transformational change at the board level and if they were willing to share their stories in a follow-up book. "Transformational governance change" was defined as the practices and strategies boards and staff had used to achieve profound cultural or governance change, and respondents were asked to be prepared to explain details on the stages of change they experienced, how challenges were addressed, who was involved, and the tools they used. At this stage of the research, respondents were offered confidentiality. Additionally, we reached out to 182 additional associations generated from personal networks, alternate lists, and a literature review of prior news stories about association board change.

These strategies produced 62 replies, of which 56 were interviewed. This figure should not be confused with a response rate, since we never identified our full "sampling frame" (i.e., the total possible number of associations that had participated in board change). Rather, this figure reflects the individuals who responded to our request, self-identified as representing boards that had experienced transformational board change, had sufficient recall of the process to participate in our study, were available within the two-month time frame we offered for an interview, responded to our e-mails, and were willing to share their stories with researchers.

Telephone interviews of 30–60 minutes were carried out with the 56 individuals, nearly all association CEOs.[1] While not all respondents ultimately described *transformational* change processes (see Chapter 2), all interviews identified at least one aspect of board change that supported the goals of this book.

Questions used in these interviews had been tested in advance and refined following a focus-group session with 12 association CEOs and management consultants in August 2013. The structured telephone interviews asked the following questions:

- What was the governance problem your association faced, and what change needed to happen?
- What were the catalysts or turning points?

---

[1] Two interviews involved the CEO and another senior manager; one included the CEO and board president; one included the CEO and the organization's external consultant.

- Who were the change agents?
- How much time has the change process taken?
- What resources, qualities, or strategies were crucial to success?
- What specific strategic tools did your association make use of?
- What was most challenging? What obstacles did you face?

Additionally, 1,261 association heads working in the Washington, D.C. and Chicago areas were invited to an alternative event, a series of four facilitated, recorded discussions conducted in May and June 2014 in D.C. and Chicago. Twenty-nine individuals attended (see Acknowledgments). An abbreviated version of the same interview questions was used.

Full transcripts from both the interviews and focus groups were analyzed by hand and with NVivo qualitative software to identify key themes, response patterns, and information that should be included in the book. The tables and figures in this book report on only the 56 full interviews, but many quotations from the larger set of 86 full and focus-group interviews are also included in the book.

Additionally, 15 of these associations were asked to participate in a second telephone interview, this time adding past or present board leaders who had been involved in the change process; 14 associations were able to participate and 18 new individuals—mainly board chairs and past chairs—were interviewed along with the original interviewees (CEOs). This material was added to the 14 cases that are included in full in this book. The inclusion criteria for selecting this smaller list of case studies were, in priority order:

1. Stories that offer the most illustrative examples of successful journeys to high-performing governance according to key themes identified in the data analysis (e.g., the change agents, catalyzing events, use of consultants, change management tools, etc.).
2. Cases that focus on real transformational change (e.g., profound culture) rather than superficial governance change (e.g., minor bylaws revisions).

3. Cases that cover the broadest amount of territory in the trade and professional associational world and offer stories and examples that readers may recognize and connect to. In this book, you will hear stories from associations representing solar power manufacturers, fraternities, summer camp professionals, estate planners, bankers, ski instructors, private school administrators, occupational therapists, realtors, caterers, nurses, and osteopaths, to name just a partial list.
4. Interview subjects were able to tell their story clearly.

Cases included in this book were edited for efficiency, tone, and chronological flow to the story. Quotes are minimally edited—the words you read are the stories we heard. Additional material pulled from association websites introduces each story to offer a fuller picture of the association's environment and mission.

Altogether, therefore, the information included in this book represents data and lessons learned from the 2013 survey of 1,585 association executive directors, plus focus groups and telephone interviews held in 2014 with 106 individuals. The data were analyzed using a "multiple case study method," which uses inductive logic to identify patterns and themes in the interviews, build theories from this data, and compare these with prior literature to identify the patterns of organizational behavior that help to explain successful governance change (Eisenhardt and Graebner 2007). In this book, two literatures are used: practitioner and academic literature on strategic change and change management, and literature on governance and boards.

Organization of This Book

This book includes two kinds of information. First, 14 original cases describe the process of governance change as it was related to us by the change agents themselves, all association leaders. The cases are organized to highlight the governance challenges these associations faced and the change management strategies they implemented. These cases are organized thematically so that they follow 10 chapters introducing conceptual material about change management and relating that material to the stories we heard.

Chapters also make generous use of quotations from the 106 individuals who participated in the focus groups or interviews. All quotes have been approved, with minimal edits, by the people we interviewed, and we thank them for their generosity and eagerness to help the association world learn from their stories. Many offered tools and resources they found instrumental to their success, and some of these can be found at the end of the book. An index is included for convenience.

Terminology Used in This Book

We recognize that nonprofit organizations use many terms to define themselves. In this book, we have aimed for consistency in terminology. When we refer to *organizations*, we mean any association or other not-for-profit membership organization, organized to promote a trade, profession, union, or other public or mutual benefit mission. We may sometimes refer to the chief staff person in this organization as the *CEO*, although many are called executive directors or hold another title. The term *board of directors* refers to the governing body with legal responsibility for the organization, although other leadership bodies may also exist and although other terms may be used to describe your board (trustees, governors).

When we refer to *governance change* we mean deliberate actions the board has taken to alter, update, or transform its fiduciary responsibilities and activities, including changes to bylaws, structure, policies, roles, activities, or expectations. Our *study participants* include any of the individuals who supported this study through interviews or focus groups.

1 | Where Does Board Change Begin?

The path to our destination is not always a straight one.
We go down the wrong road, we get lost, we turn back.
Maybe it doesn't matter which road we embark on.
Maybe what matters is that we embark.

—Barbara Hall, writer and producer

Every change starts with a thought, and very often, the thought is framed as a question:

Why isn't this working?
How can we make something better?
What if we did this differently?

In nonprofit governance, the critical point when change begins can arise out of challenges—situational or chronic—to a board's performance. A board member may think:

"Something is not right on this board."
"Why can't we get more done?"
"I like serving on this board except for _____."
"I'm not making a difference. Perhaps I should resign."
"Why do my ideas seem so out of place?"
"Everyone keeps telling me, 'We've always done it this way. . . .'"

Our interviews found that association CEOs and board members shared similar thoughts to these. Even when the cause was hard to pin down, expressing the thought helped get the conversation started:

"There were problems. You would hear things."
"When I was hiring, prospective staff would ask specific questions about board involvement."
"It had been brewing under the surface."
"We had organizational misalignment."
"The board was not able to make decisions."
"We were losing members."
"The board was exhausted."

In other instances, our interview subjects clearly knew where problems resided:

"All the decisions were being made in the back room."
"The board was spending all its time on 'administrivia.'"
"In learned societies the board chair is the highest person in the field at the time and it's an honorific."
"The board spent a lot of time discussing issues that weren't really in their purview."
"There was no direction. We were living in the past. We were the world's largest association of x—and we were stuck."

"It was an operational board. We had budget meetings that lasted eight to 12 hours. We had board discussions about how to price a manual."

From the awareness that something is not right comes intention to do something about it. Researcher and lecturer Joe Dispenza observes, "Intention involves directing the mind, with purpose and efficacy, toward some object or outcome." Moving from awareness of a need to a plan of action—to *planned change*—is important to successful change because it's the only way to maintain control over the outcome. This book, after all, is about creating the change we want by taking action, avoiding the change we don't want by simply letting it happen.

Concepts and Application

What kind of change can happen at the board level when problems are *not* addressed? What are the risks of passivity, of thinking these problems will work themselves out on their own, perhaps through board member turnover? One probable outcome is that the most valuable people, who recognize the problems, get frustrated and quit.

Comparing responses from ASAE's 2013 Governance Survey, we find that the cost of doing nothing is pretty scary. Association executive directors were much more likely to consider quitting when they worked for associations with boards they judged to be low performing (Gazley and Bowers 2013). The lowest-ranked associations also had twice the turnover in other executive staff compared to associations with high-performing boards.

Like staff, board members also vote with their feet. High-performing association boards had more stable board memberships. But associations with low-performing boards were three times as likely to report either greater or less-than-optimal board member turnover. They were twice as likely to report difficulty in recruiting

Table 1.1 Comparison of High- and Low-Performing Boards (2013 ASAE Governance Survey)

	Top 25% of Ranked Association Boards, Based on CEO Board Performance Rating	Bottom 25% of Ranked Association Boards, Based on CEO Board Performance Rating	Total Average of All Boards (*n* = 1,585)
CEO intends to leave	37%	54%	44%
High staff turnover, affecting more than half of key positions	8%	18%	12%
Board has greater turnover than optimal	3%	10%	6%
Board has less turnover than optimal	9%	31%	17%
Difficult to recruit board members	49%	85%	66%
Association membership is growing	48%	24%	36%
Association budget is growing	55%	33%	46%
Association membership is shrinking	16%	38%	25%
Association budget is shrinking	16%	30%	21%

new board members. And these associations had much weaker membership and fiscal health.

These data also suggest that the first sign of a need for board change may not be self-evident, but may emerge as something entirely different. Without initially connecting the problem to leadership, the organization may recognize that it is not healthy financially, or that internal processes don't seem to be working. From our interviews, we heard:

> "Membership was flat; programs were not growing."
>
> "I met with the board chair, and we both expressed dissatisfaction with my annual review process. So we began to have this discussion. . . ."
>
> "There had been a number of short-term strategic plans. It was easy to kick the can down the road. We would take markers, not hit them, and then do a new strategic plan. There was frustration at not being able to grow."
>
> "Our industry was at a crossroads."
>
> "It was clear to me that one of the reasons for the financial crisis was rooted in the structure and function of the board of directors. The organization was basically not doing anything but spinning in a circle, depending on who was pulling the hardest."
>
> "We did not have productive relationships with our colleague associations."
>
> "There was growing member concern about _____" [safety, growth, professionalization, fiscal health, relevancy, etc.].

Understanding the Nature of Change

As Tom Peters so succinctly put it, "Innovate or die." Governance leaders can benefit from understanding theories of change generally, which can then be applied to the context of boards and governance systems. Todd Jick writes in *Managing Change* (1993) that there are no surefire instructions for successful change. But the process of change has some common characteristics—and that's where theory comes in.

Please don't get nervous as we introduce the *t*-word. Theories, after all, are simply descriptions of how the real world works—conceptual models that are built from patterns of real organizational and human behavior. The strongest theories earn their keep because they not only help to explain what happened but also help us predict what might happen next.

Theories of change are extraordinarily useful to people who are experiencing change or trying to figure out how to get change started. Change instills hope, optimism, passion, and energy in people, but it can also be frustrating, threatening, stressful, confusing, and messy. So theories of change help those who are just embarking, as well as those who are in the midst of change, understand what they are experiencing and what the roadmap might look like for getting it right. They reassure everyone involved in a change process, whether an agent of change or a recipient, that others have gone down this road before them.

Types of Change

Change takes many forms. Change may occur due to growth or a leadership transition, be proactive or reactive in nature, be unplanned or planned. Rune Todnem By (2005) observes that change can be structural, remedial, evolutionary, revolutionary, and radical. It can occur as a result of internal or external events, rules or legislative change, strategy deployment, consolidations, mergers or acquisitions, restructuring or downsizing. Change can be continuous or incremental, fundamental or minor, slow or rapid.

In this book, many (although not all) of our interview subjects described **transformational changes** to their board. *Transformational change* is the term for far-reaching and radical alterations (to culture, leadership, mission fulfillment) where the future state of the organization may only be imagined and the path may be unclear (Jick 1993).

Incremental and less radical changes also occur in organizational systems through developmental or transitional adjustments. Governance improvements may involve all three forms of change, as organizational leaders may decide to entirely reinvent their board culture and decision-making rules while still retaining what they already do well. In this book, we find association leaders describing examples of many kinds of change, only some of which ultimately can be considered transformational.

The models and theories of change, built on observation of the world of organizational dynamics, are numerous. We discuss just a few in this chapter, focusing on those that help us understand how to *manage* change. Yet, even in such a rich and varied field, change theories hold some characteristics in common. They all describe change as a **process** of **action planning** whose distinct elements must be managed (see Lewin's Planned Change Model in Figure 1.1). They also observe the need for information-gathering, **diagnosis, and learning** as part of that process (see the Action Research and Positive Models, also in Figure 1.1). Experts also agree that change has a high likelihood of failure, so that efforts must receive sufficient **support** and resources to be successful (Balogun and Hope Hailey 2008; By 2005). Finally, many models also note that a crucial element in supporting successful change is understanding and effectively addressing **human reactions** to change (see the Habit Loop described in Chapter 2).

Change Models

The models briefly described here each contribute to our understanding of how organizations successfully create a **process of diagnosis and learning, action planning, and support for the people affected by change**. We also relate these models to board dynamics and the experiences that our interview subjects described. (See Figure 1.1.)

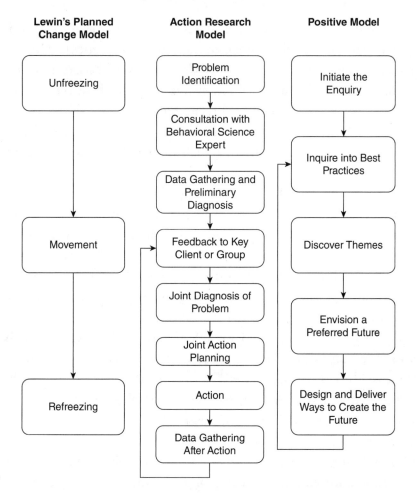

Figure 1.1 Comparison of Planned Change Models
Source: Cummings and Worley (2015). Republished with permission of South-Western College Publishing; permission conveyed through Copyright Clearance Center.

Lewin's Planned Change Model

Kurt Lewin, a 1950s psychologist, characterized change as a three-stage process. In the first stage, "unfreezing," refers to the raising of consciousness that change needs to happen, and the effort to build the case and motivation for change. One key tool or resource to support "unfreezing" is to introduce information that shows discrepancies between behaviors desired and behaviors currently exhibited in a group or organization. The second, "movement," stage is where action happens, where new ways of doing and behaving occur. "Freezing" is the third stage, which is the habituation or institution-alization of the change (Cummings and Worley 2009). "Freezing" doesn't mean that an organization stops growing, but rather that the new behaviors are accepted and institutionalized.

Action Research Model

Elaborating on Lewin's model is the notion of planned change as a cyclical process in which initial research about the organization provides information to guide subsequent action (Cummings and Worley 2009). Action research is traditionally aimed both at helping specific organiza-tions implement planned change and at developing more general knowledge that can be applied to other settings (Shani and Bushe 1987; Susman and Evered 1978). Thus, action research often involves an outside consultant to bring new knowledge to the organization.

1. **Problem identification:** The *aha* moment that includes a lead-er's awareness that bringing in an organizational development (OD) practitioner might be helpful to solve a problem.
2. **Consultation with a behavioral science expert:** Leader and practitioner assessment of the state of the organization and the opportunities for change.
3. **Data gathering and preliminary diagnosis:** Data gathering through interviews, process observation, questionnaires, and organi-zational performance data; preliminary diagnosis by the OD practi-tioner. In OD, any action by the OD practitioner can be viewed as an intervention that will have some effect on the organization.
4. **Feedback to a key client or group:** The OD practitioner provides the client with the data along with analysis and/or initial recommendations.

5. **Joint diagnosis of the problem:** The collaborative process between the client and the OD practitioner to ensure that interpretations of the data are understood and meaningful in order to develop a consensus statement of the problem(s) to be addressed.

6. **Joint action planning:** The client and the OD practitioner collaboratively developing a change action plan.

7. **Action:** Implementation of the action plan. This may include installing new methods and procedures, reorganizing structures and work designs, and reinforcing new behaviors.

8. **Data gathering after action:** Because action research is a cyclical process, data must also be gathered to measure the effects of the action and to feed the results back to the organization. This effort in turn may result in re-diagnosis and new actions, such as a return to a previous step (Cummings and Worley 2009).

The Positive Model

The Positive Model focuses on what the organization is doing right. It helps members understand what doesn't need to be fixed (Cummings and Worley 2009, p. 28). By identifying and acknowledging the positive behaviors and capacities an organization already possesses, leaders can use these qualities to support a future change process. Positive models also provide balance since the natural inclination in organizational development efforts is to focus on what is not working. Experts observe that while questions that focus on challenges and deficiencies (e.g., "What needs to be fixed?") are valid, an excessive focus on dysfunctions can actually cause organizations to become worse or fail to improve (Seligman 2002).

We will employ aspects of the Positive Model in Chapter 4. The steps of the model are:

1. **Initiate the inquiry:** The process of getting the members to address change. Emphasis is on member involvement to identify the organizational issue they have the most energy to address. This helps to create organizational ownership for the change being addressed.

2. **Inquire into best practices:** The collection of the internal stories regarding the successes and changes that have already been achieved, and using these as models or examples for future change opportunities regarding the organizational issue they wish to address.

3. **Discover themes:** Taking those stories and analyzing them for the themes (i.e., commonalities of experience and underlying mechanisms) to provide evidence and inspiration as a basis for the next step.

4. **Envision a preferred future:** Based on the internal stories of best practices and identified themes, members are then encouraged to collectively visualize the organization's future and develop "possibility propositions"—statements that bridge the organizational current best practices with ideal possibilities for future organization. From that information, relevant stakeholders and organizational processes are identified that will require alignment to create the future vision.

5. **Design and deliver ways to create the future:** The process of creating an action plan to create the future vision (Cummings and Worley 2009).

Applying the Positive Model to what we learned in our interviews, many association leaders described a process of appreciative inquiry to identify not only what needed to be changed but also the positive qualities they already possessed that would support successful change. Those qualities included strong cultures of learning and self-assessment, a healthy reserve of trust between staff and the board, or a culture of adaptation because it was the nature of the industry or profession they were in. For example, Peg Smith, CEO of the American Camp Association, describes a crucial decision point when she had to rely on her association's culture to move forward:

I had built a good deal of social capital to take the organization to the next step. We had done all the buffing and polishing that we could and I knew we had to go to the next step to really make change. I also knew that we had a board president at the time who had the right competency, attitude, and credibility in the community to make it happen. When I first presented the "call to action" it was eerily quiet. I was very worried—I blew all my social capital in one fell swoop. Then the conversation started.

Change and Life-Cycle Theories

Many of the executive directors and board chairs we interviewed described the need to update their governance structure as the organization achieved a new level of maturity. We heard many stories in our interviews about how an organization's growth or decline was propelling the need for governance change. Change may occur as a natural part of organizational evolution, a response to growth, decline, new needs, or opportunities. Young organizations change to survive, to claim a niche, or to reach the next level of growth. Mature organizations change to reenergize or renew their cultures, or to rid themselves of calcified cultures that prevent them from market adaptation (Beatty and Ulrich 1993, p. 61).

Not surprisingly, then, many of our stories come from well-established associations—some approaching their third century—that found change was needed to remain relevant. But somewhat surprising is that not all stories of change in our book occurred in response to competitive pressures (see more in Chapter 3). In some cases, the associations were thriving but recognized that future health—their ability to prevent a future shock—required a different outlook on governance. David Harvey's story from the Society of Estate and Trust Practitioners (see Chapter 2) will illustrate this point.

This perspective on change is important because an organization's evolutionary path or life cycle can dictate not only the *why* of change but also the *how*. Figure 1.2 helps to explain not only what might be at stake—strategies, power, values, and so forth—but also the central role that executive leadership plays in driving change or any other strategic reorientation (Tushman and Romanelli 2009).

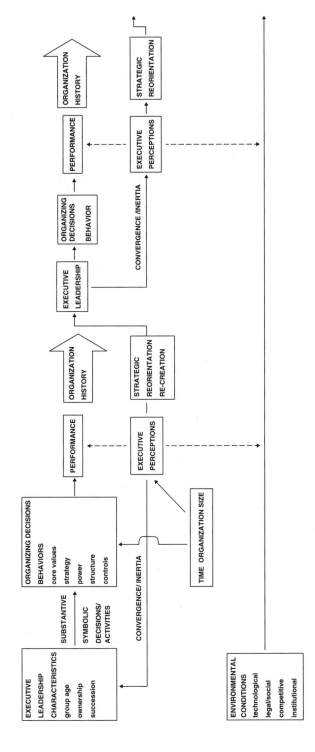

Figure 1.2 Organization Evolution: A Schematic Model

Source: M. Tushman and E. Romanelli, "Organizational Evolution: A Metamorphosis of Convergence and Reorientation," *Research in Organizational Behavior: An Annual Series of Analytical Essays and Critical Reviews* 7 (1985): 171–222.

Summary

In their statements, we may not immediately see association leaders making connections between organizational health and the health of the board. But each of these individuals told us they understood, sooner or later, that their board leadership, composition, consciousness, and/or processes needed to change if they were to tackle the larger organizational needs identified earlier. This sentiment became a consistent theme in our study—that governance improvements were about more than board-specific needs. These changes were required to secure the future of the entire organization.

A consistent theme in our study [was] that governance improvements were about more than board-specific needs. These changes were required to secure the future of the entire organization.

The theories of change we introduced help explain that change can be predictable even when it seems quite the opposite. Change affects individuals in ways that knowledgeable associations can predict, as Chapter 2 will explain. Board changes may be triggered by mostly foreseeable events, as Chapter 3 will describe. And managing change involves systematic processes of diagnosis and learning, action planning, and support for the people affected by change. Perhaps most encouraging to those facing governance change is that many resources, tools, and strategies are available to support a healthy change process (covered in Chapters 4 and beyond).

2 | Change and People

People don't resist change. They resist being changed!
—Peter Senge, systems scientist and lecturer

The full story of governance change at the Southwest Association of Episcopal Schools follows Chapter 4. When Connie Wootton, executive director, recalled the journey her board took, she focused especially on how they facilitated a general comfort with the change process:

We feared the change because we were pretty comfortable. But because we were talking about sweeping changes and because we would lose some longstanding board members, we spent the better part of three years easing into this. It wasn't angering [board members] that worried us, but hurting them. Change is frightening. But we realized we still had ten fingers and ten toes, so then we could think about other changes. We were determined we would take it slowly to do the least harm.

This story illustrates nicely that managing change is ultimately about managing people. Change is ultimately a cognitive process. Understanding and actively managing this idea is often a key determinant in how rocky the road of change will be.

Concepts and Application

Change Agents

Individuals do not all assume the same roles in the change process (Jick 1993). Some people are change recipients. Others are change agents, serving as active drivers of a change process. These are the people whose stories you will hear in many of our case studies.

Analysis of our interviews,[1] presented in Table 2.1, finds that the change agents who initiated a board transformation included five sources. In frequency order, change was initiated by (1) the board as a whole or a group of board members, (2) executive directors or CEOs, (3) a CEO and board working together, (4) the board chair or president, and (5) the membership, portions of the membership, or sections or chapters. In Table 2.1, we credit to the board of directors (rather than CEO) any cases where the board may have deliberately hired a new CEO as a change agent, since we reasoned that the board still made the decision to initiate change.

One thing is clear from this analysis: While board members may be the most frequent agents of change and while a healthy amount of change in our case studies came through joint board–staff action, organizations must also be prepared for pressure from members to change. In our interviews, change initiated by members was infrequent but included both mature organizations facing changing member

---

[1] This table includes the leaders of the 53 (of 56) associations who could recall this information.

Table 2.1 Change Agents in Association Governance

Change Agent	Examples	Reported Frequency
Board of directors	Boards may recognize the need for change as a whole, or a cohort of board members may run on a "change ticket." New board members with prior governance experience may pressure the other members for change.	33%
CEO/ executive director	New CEOs often bring new knowledge and perspectives with them, recognizing the need for board change before the board does.	23%
Joint board/ CEO action	Change may begin in joint discussions between the full board and staff leadership. CEOs and board chairs may also agree jointly that change is needed.	21%
Chair	Longstanding board leaders may act out of frustration; new board leaders may act when they bring new knowledge and perspectives with them. Given their leadership role, they may also recognize the need for board change before other members do.	19%
Membership	Members may respond to a crisis by demanding board change. They may demand new member benefits as an organization grows, triggering a realization that the board model is inadequate for a growing organization. They may pressure the board for change out of concerns about organizational direction. Changing member demographics may pressure a board to reinvent itself.	4%

demographics and young organizations facing member demand for more services.

Some change agents we interviewed accelerated the process by strategically recruiting new individuals to their board who could serve as change agents. This strategy is described in both cases that follow this chapter (Society of Trust and Estate Practitioners; American Occupational Therapy Association). New board members also helped to foster a more detached and objective conversation within the board about how the board's restructuring would affect their roles.

Recipients of Change

Some individuals are recipients rather than agents of change. Board members and staff can serve as both the drivers and the recipients of new governance expectations. Research tells us that recipients of change can express dramatic emotions when change is forced upon them, even when the promised change is positive (Argyris 1993; Jick 1993). Recipients of change may be concerned about how the new ideas will affect their status and responsibilities. Many of our cases in this book describe instances where staff, members, or board members felt threatened by governance change, resulting at times in strong emotional reactions.

Scholars of organizational development and change (ODC) use cognitive theories of human behavior to observe that resistance to change may have valid roots, since it reflects a fairly normal human desire for the familiar and routine. Letting go of old habits for new ways of doing things introduces ambiguity, and ambiguity can be frightening. As Peg Smith, CEO of the American Camp Association, observed in her interview with us:

None of the books prepare you for the need for psychological hardiness. No one is talking about what you have to be steeled for.

There are moments when you really doubt what you have started. Change frightens people and people hate ambiguity.

An individual can resist change not necessarily because he dislikes the new strategy but because he is reacting to the need to adapt and the perceived loss of control over his present situation (Jick 1993, pp. 6, 324). Andrew Davidson, CEO of the Oregon Association of Hospitals and Health Systems, described the experience:

Besides myself, there were other people who saw the need for change. Everybody who wasn't on the executive committee wanted change but didn't feel any sense of control over what was happening. They weren't driving the train.

A change recipient's negative reaction to what seems to be a promising idea may surprise the agents of change when they know the organization will be the better for it, but it occurs because human reactions to any form of change are closely related to our reactions to loss. So the human emotions of the grieving process—shock, denial, followed by acknowledgment and adaptation—can also occur as change recipients adjust to new goals, cultures, and expectations within organizations (Jick 1993).

The agents of board change should understand that they will not only have to manage its structural aspects, they will also have to help board members, staff, and the organization's membership adapt emotionally and cognitively. In what follows, we discuss two strategies that our subjects employed to help manage change: organizational culture and emotional intelligence.

Using Organizational Culture to Support Recipients of Change

Some associations we talked to seized the opportunity to use an already healthy culture to support the change process. These were often the cases that reported the easiest governance transitions. Compare, for example, the two quotations below:

1. "There was a tradition of no change, a mindset that 'if it produced me, it must be good.' So we got some resistance from board and staff."
2. "Our culture worked for us. The board was always open to change."

In the first instance, the change process took four years and some effort due to a conservative professional culture that valued consistency. It's normal to expect some professions to react to change less dynamically than others might. Ultimately, this association's leaders anticipated the possibility of resistance and planned for it to achieve the improvements they sought.

In the second instance, Mark Dorsey, CAE, who is CEO of the Professional Ski Instructors of America (PSIA) and the American Association of Snowboard Instructors (AASI), described a change process of about a year and a half in which the board worked effectively in partnership with staff to restructure itself, delegated responsibly, and "owned" the solutions. He credits the successful governance restructuring they accomplished to an association culture where board members were focused and asked "the tough strategic questions."

The point is that in the end, both of these cases were success stories because leaders worked with and through, rather than against, their prevailing cultures.

Using Emotional Intelligence to Support Recipients of Change

Experts also suggest that change agents who are skilled in emotional intelligence—the human ability to monitor one's own emotional state and those of others—will be most successful at supporting recipients of change as they adjust to a new set of expectations (Huy 1999). Organizations can invest at the institutional level in building their capacity to manage the emotional aspects of change. This institutional "emotional capability" in turn offers change recipients the empathy, time, support, positive reinforcement, and information they need to adjust to change. This point is illustrated in Connie Wootton's story at the start of this chapter.

Emotional capability is also built through experience at successful change in the past. Even minor successes produce residual feelings of self-efficacy and make leaders bolder at tackling new challenges. Organizations should look for opportunities to celebrate any successful changes. Dale Brown, CAE, president and CEO of Financial Services Institute, observed how his board became more effective over time by building a "culture that is very trusting of each other through relationship building." Victoria Ceh, MPA, of the International Society of Hair Restoration Surgery, described an organization in which "we play hard and we work hard." In his former role as executive director at Delta Sigma Phi, Scott Wiley, CAE, observed, "There has to be an element of fun. At the end of day, people want to be part of something bigger than themselves, something they can look back on positively and warmly." And Christine Todd, CAE, of the Northern Virginia Association of REALTORS® recalled,

> I was worried that I was always giving them bad news. So at the end of the year at one of our conventions we made it really fun-filled. And the board at the time said, "Chris, we needed this so badly." This was a huge lesson for me—give them a break, have fun.

Habitualizing Change

Organizational change and development experts suggest that change takes root as change recipients get used to a new way of doing things.

Individuals in the change process (members, board members, past board members, external constituents, the public, staff) will all need to be shepherded along in a deliberate and caring manner until there is critical mass and momentum to habitualize the change. And then the organization itself will need to habitualize the new routines to create the desired change outcomes. Connie Wootton's story, given earlier, helps to explain why this strategy works.

In *The Power of Habit: Why We Do What We Do in Life and Business,* Charles Duhigg (2012) distills prior research to explain how individuals and organizations change habits. In case after case, from champion athletes to workers in the London Underground to activists in the Montgomery Bus Boycott, from corporations to hospitals, Duhigg explains how individual and organizational habits are changed through use of the Habit Loop (Figure 2.1).

Habitual cues result from either a gradual awareness of something not working or triggers, each of which can be boiled down into one or more of the following: location, time, emotional state, other people,

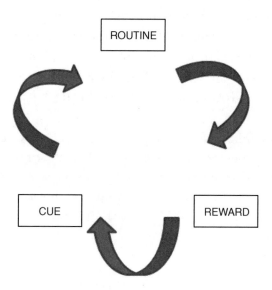

Figure 2.1   The Habit Loop
Source: Duhigg (2012). Republished with permission of Random House.

and an immediately preceding action. When you actively become aware of those cues or triggers and the default behaviors that are prompted (seemingly automatic, rarely reflected upon) that lead to previous rewards, then creating a plan that anticipates cues and choosing alternative behaviors can deliver a different reward (a new, preferred outcome).

We found in our interviews many cases of organizations engaged in governance patterns who told us "it had always been done that way." Applying the Habit Loop to board change, a change agent can challenge organizational or governance habits by actively introducing new cues and rewards. For example, in our consulting work, we once encountered an association with an unusual set of bylaws and asked, "Why does your organization have board positions for both a chair and a president in your bylaws?" It turned out no one had ever considered that question or could remember why it was included in the bylaws of this 50-plus-year-old association. When the board considered the work involved to manage the two roles with their overlapping responsibilities and to keep track of who was doing what, the directors easily recognized that there was an opportunity to revisit this. The cue was to create the understanding that "perhaps we don't need to do it this way," and the outcome was a reward in the more efficient and productive use of volunteer board time and energy the organization could enjoy.

In the context of governance, then, a cue can be either slow, gradual awareness, perhaps helped along by questions from an objective outsider or board newcomer, or it can be a trigger resulting from an internal or external event. Boards that desire to move along the journey toward high performance have an opportunity to pay special attention to possible cues and triggers. The rewards that come from the outcomes of awareness and reevaluation and the possibility of applying or adopting something new create the culture of change and a new way of being or doing—a new normal.

Change is really about behaving in a new way, largely as a result of changing a habit. And changing habits is hard. Phillippa Lally, a health psychology researcher at University College London, studied healthy habit formation among 82 people over a 12-week period. Subjects chose simple habits like "drinking a bottle of water with lunch" or more difficult tasks like "running for 15 minutes before dinner." While Lally found that on average, subjects took about two months before a new behavior became automatic, the total time to habit acquisition ranged widely from 28 to 115 days. This study is important to our discussion in emphasizing that some board members, volunteers, staff, and members require more time to adjust to new governance processes. Governance experts suggest introducing proposed changes incrementally, repeatedly emphasizing and practicing new governance processes, and actively managing the process (see Chapter 4 for more).

Summary

This chapter helps us understand how people experience change emotionally and cognitively. In Chapter 3 we discuss further the strategies that association leaders used to help individuals adjust emotionally to new expectations.

Awareness of the need for change is often not lacking. We may know what's wrong even though we can't seem to get it fixed. Consultants often report that their job sometimes is simply lending authority and credibility to help develop traction to address an issue that some in the organization have already identified as a problem.

Establishing consensus that the change is needed and finding the right path toward better practices, and then making it happen, can stump many organizations that operate by default. It's not necessarily a "we've always done it this way" consciousness that stumps organizational leaders; it is also basic subconscious programming and lack of overall awareness (not everyone knows what they don't know) that sometimes makes us blind to the influence of ingrained detrimental activities, operations, or behaviors.

Working with a specific change model helps to engage the recipients of change successfully because it can decouple the emotional aspects of the change response while at the same time teaching a new way of understanding an organizational problem. Broaching the subject in the boardroom can be difficult because there can be a tendency for board members to take the suggestion as a personal attack on their leadership abilities. But broaching these practices as something reflective of the increasing sophistication and professionalization of the nonprofit sector can make the process nonthreatening and the results empowering.

The stories of the Society of Trust and Estate Practitioners and the American Occupational Therapy Association that follow describe cases where board members recognized the need for change but had to work through its more emotional implications first. As the cases illustrate, methodically and diligently working with a change model helps bring everyone along during the process.

Leveraging Culture to Create an Efficient Governing Board

Case: Society of Trust and Estate Practitioners

 Being a global, healthy, highly respected association serving a rapidly evolving profession doesn't mean you are immune to resistance from the "old guard." Learn how one association used its culture of consensual association to create a nimbler and more efficient governing board.

Founded in London in 1991, the mission of the Society of Trust and Estate Practitioners (STEP) is to help families plan their assets across generations by educating professionals and promoting high standards, connecting advisors and families globally, informing public policy, and acting in the public

(continued)

(*continued*)

interest. The society has grown quickly, with local branches established first in England and Wales and then spreading to the rest of the UK and Commonwealth before expanding to Europe, Canada, the Caribbean and beyond. By 2000, STEP had developed into a full-scale worldwide professional association (www.step.org).

The changes for the Society of Trust and Estate Practitioners—a more strategically engaged and nimbler board—didn't happen overnight. As Chief Executive David Harvey recalls, it was a long and sometimes painful process, but it yielded great results.

> I had been in public affairs within the industry for 13 years before taking on the CEO role at STEP. The association was clubby before I arrived. If you worked in a traditional accounting practice, there really wasn't that much professional management. There was enormous expertise (the best lawyers, the best accountants, the best people working on philanthropic giving) but the idea that there needed to be a manager who would make that business successful was quite slow coming.

But "winds of change" helped STEP along. By 2008, their membership had doubled to 12,000. Smaller practices were merging into larger professional firms. STEP's access to bigger banks and new areas of expertise (e.g., on elder care) added to a culture that would support a higher standard of operation.

Challenge: Reluctance to Change

But efforts to change were slowed by a cautious professional culture. David Harvey recalls,

There was a reluctance to change among the senior members of the council (STEP's governing body). Some didn't want to lose their power. There needed to be better governance for the sake of being effective for our members. And our governance had to reflect the global nature of our business.

Almost all our members were lawyers and chartered accountants, which meant they had a particular background. And we are a [fiscally conservative] organization. But professional development education was soaring. We had more revenue and more freedom to do things. We looked at how satisfied members were, their participation levels, their wants. And it became clear that satisfaction was high but future satisfaction was not guaranteed if we didn't do something. That was quite persuasive.

Satisfaction was high but future satisfaction was not guaranteed if we didn't do something.

Challenge: Large, Slow-Moving Board

At that time STEP was governed by a globally elected 40-member governance council. All committees had to go the council for major decisions. But the council only met three or four times a year. Harvey described the problem:

We were having trouble making decisions. We did have a smaller management council of six members, but they wouldn't take action for fear that the governance council would overrule them. We asked, "How do we take the next step?" We had to learn that governance was not just a lawyer's view of "all about the rules." It was also about strategy.

(*continued*)

(continued)

Michael Young, immediate past chair of the board, helped to implement this strategy:

> This wasn't a very satisfactory model for governing a very substantial body. It was very difficult to be a representative in a parliamentary sense, to consult members in time before a vote. We needed to be light on our feet and be more nimble to make rapid decisions. We decided to do a top-to-bottom review of our governance and committee structure.

Strategy: Agree to Change

STEP's change agents began by convincing the council members that better governance was necessary for the society to keep its momentum. Agreement on the need to change was swiftly accomplished given the society's tradition of collecting member satisfaction data. However, the next step required council members to relinquish some of their traditional operational authority.

Challenge: Relinquish Powers

Young observed, from his point of view as a board member:

> It was going to be a major change for the council members because their role was effectively to run the staff. I could see it from their perspective as volunteers; they made the commitment to be elected with an expectation that they would have an active and interesting role, participating in all the vital decision making

for STEP. Come this review, we were asking council to give up all those powers and vest them in a board that would be loosely answerable to council but not controlled by council except that the council votes the members into office and would have the power to review them. So for some people it was going to be a somewhat painful decision to go from a highly active role to a more consultative role.

Strategy: Get Objective Advice

Discussions within the council were slow and painful. Harvey recalls:

One of our members had the courage to stand up and say, "Let's be frank. This process isn't working." There was a broad view that we needed a structure to the process. We needed an outsider who could be the black sheep if need be.

We agreed to have an external advisor who would take the council with some other added guests through a series of review meetings of over a year. The consultant was the objective outsider who told us we had not really grown up. He highlighted what wasn't working. We eventually identified the issues that required attention. We established working parties on key difficult topics. Everyone had a chance to talk.

Strategy: Support Open Discussion

STEP's process focused on discussion and reviews of benchmarking data from ASAE and the Professional Association Research Network. As Harvey described it:

(continued)

(continued)

We gave smart people as much access as we could to how other associations did things. We didn't say one thing was right or wrong. The vision was toward better decision making.

Strategy: Use Data

Young outlined the process:

One committee examined every aspect of STEP's governance. Their recommendations were modeled after corporate entities, such as having a governing board with the responsibility for running the organization; a council that was more akin to a consultative body with more defined decision-making responsibilities; and a series of committees covering specialty areas also with more defined decision-making responsibilities.

Dealing with the structural and policies issues—that was quite easy. But giving up roles—that was not.

Harvey added: "Dealing with a lot of the structural and policies issues and what we should do—that was quite easy. But giving up roles—that was not. This took quite a bit longer to get through."

Young agreed:

Some people felt uncomfortable. There was sweat and even pain along the way. Not sure I want to remember it. But it is an awful lot better now. Governance wasn't what excited them; the driver has always been about learning and education. One major driver in achieving consensus was a fundamental realization: If anything went drastically wrong in STEP, it would be the council members who would go to jail. The realization that these risks existed helped them give up that power and see that governance had to be concentrated in a much smaller board.

Strategy: Pace the Change

Harvey observed the need for a measured pace:

We didn't try to do it all at once. We said to the existing council members, "You will get the rest of your term. You will be respected." We took our time to build shared respect and buy-in for the new ideas. We were lucky we were not in a crisis situation. We had recognized the need for change before change was desperately needed. It's harder to enact change when it's forced upon you.

> *We didn't try to do it all at once. We said to the existing council members, "You will get the rest of your term. You will be respected."*

Strategy: Shrink the Board

In the end, STEP agreed on a council of 30 members and a governing board of eight, including the CEO serving *ex officio*. Previously, "people wouldn't rock the boat in a larger group." With a smaller board, "members feel more empowered to speak out."

(continued)

(*continued*)
Strategy: Recruit Change Agents

The 10 extra council members were persuaded to step down; one was forced out. David Harvey acknowledges the risk, since the change agents could have been the same members who were willing to step down, causing a loss of momentum. But STEP also enlisted other unofficial change agents to play a role in the implementation. Some council members who were not threatened by the change joined in. They helped to foster a more detached discussion about the repercussions for the council. Young explained:

> With some of our leading figures there has always been a personal culture of measuring and reassessing. So our mission was to move that culture to other people not from that background. [In board recruitment], we looked for people who would be good change agents.

With the benefit of hindsight, David Harvey has made some surprising conclusions about the transition to a nimbler global board:

> What we thought would be most challenging was the five-year planning. But we had consensus already on our plan. What was most challenging really was getting it done. When you have a board increasingly far apart geographically, it is hard work to make it gel. The board's composition has become more global. We have to work to help to improve learning curves. We have to manage this more intelligently.

Taking the Long View on Governance Change

Case: *American Occupational Therapy Association, Inc.*

 When Fred Somers was brought in to address a declining membership, he didn't realize he and AOTA's board were embarking on a 10-year effort to ensure the association was aligned with modern legal governance expectations. But that's what they achieved. In the process this board not only learned to lead itself, it learned a lot about effective member communication and taking the long view on governance change.

Established in 1917, the American Occupational Therapy Association (AOTA) is a national professional association. Its mission is to advance the quality, availability, use, and support of occupational therapy through standard setting, advocacy, education, and research on behalf of its members and the public. Current AOTA membership is approximately 50,000, including occupational therapists, therapy assistants, and students.

Strategy: Early Wins

The board's first restructuring strategy, some 10 years ago, was to end its constituency-based model and shrink its size. People sat on the board by virtue of their other roles and responsibilities (chairs of "sections"). They were bringing their constituency priorities to the board, and that was not working. The solution was a reorganized board of four officers and six at-large directors elected by the membership. To offer the board more perspective, two "public" members—a consumer representative and a public representative—are appointed by the incoming board president.

(continued)

(continued)

Challenge: Declining Membership

Frederick P. Somers, executive director of AOTA since 2004, has been with the association for 29 years in different positions. Somers described the association he inherited:

> I've been here for good times, bad times, and good times again. I came in when the profession itself was undergoing major change. AOTA had previously had a 60,000-person membership base, followed by declines of about 7.5 percent annually for five or six years, and then in 2004 the board selected me as the new CEO. One of my first tasks was to address the membership challenge. The membership challenge was central to everything else.

In 2006, AOTA created a new strategic vision:

> **AOTA's Centennial Vision**—*We envision that occupational therapy is a powerful, widely recognized, science-driven, and evidence-based profession with a globally connected and diverse workforce meeting society's occupational needs.*

One of Somers's first hires was AOTA's chief operating officer, Christopher Bluhm, who joined the conversation:

> We are coming up on the one-hundredth anniversary of the founding of the profession. The year 2017 will be a big one and our strategic thinking about our Centennial Vision for AOTA helped focus the organization overall. In addition, the board started creating ad-hoc groups that met on a regular basis to discuss specific generative topics. These groups were more nimble than traditional standing bodies and were time-limited with built-in sunsets. Those two things happening at about the same time really have contributed to the success of the new governance model.

Challenge: Split Governance

After changes to the board, alignment of other governing bodies needed review. The association still faced a challenge familiar to the association world—a split governance system. Bluhm recalled:

One area that needed attention was the role of the representative assembly, comprising 85 people elected by members in each state. Its authority had evolved over time, creating responsibility overlap with the governing board. Originally created as the legislative body to address professional policy making, it was now addressing issues that went well beyond its original charter and often into operations, confusing its role. Our governing board did not have the authority to change certain things because of the evolved role of the representative assembly; many issues had to go back to the representative assembly for approval.

The added agenda items used precious time in a group that only met face-to-face once a year and diminished their ability to focus on policy, to respond quickly to emerging matters, or to establish the clear lines of fiduciary responsibility to which boards are held under state nonprofit law.

Strategy: Align Governance Needs with Mission

The first big attempt at change came in 2009. Bluhm described what happened first:

(continued)

(*continued*)

The board had a number of discussions about how our governance structures and processes might be aligned to facilitate greater
membership participation and better reflect best practice for
association governance. We used the Centennial Vision we
had developed to prioritize and frame the discussions, and to
stay focused on the strategic level.

Strategy: Create a Process for Change

Next, an ad-hoc committee was initiated by the board, with the
charge: "To undertake a comprehensive review of current
methods and processes that support member participation in
the Association, including governance . . . and to assess the
participation needs and desires of members and models for
participation . . ." The board was very careful about the composition of the committee, mindful of historical relationships
between the board and the assembly.

*Part of the difficulty we faced was a
general feeling of "Why change
what's not broken?"*

So AOTA deliberately
brought in stakeholders from
every side, choosing, for example, a former speaker of the
assembly to chair the process.

Challenge: How to Build Momentum

Bluhm observed:

Part of the difficulty we faced was a general feeling of "Why
change what's not broken?" But some also perceived a prospective
loss of voice in governing the association. Furthermore, the

assembly met once a year and turned over by a third each year. Contextual knowledge of the changes we tried to make was lost each year and the new members tended to look to the leaders who were still there who really didn't want change. We couldn't build up a critical mass of change champions.

Strategy: Obtain Expertise

Bluhm observed that he oversaw the membership function, where AOTA needed to find ways to continue momentum:

We had brought in a consultant to survey the members (satisfaction, direction, interaction, what they expected, and what kind of participation they wanted given how the world is changing). We got into the whole issue of governance through the lens of engagement. We looked at how technology has changed the nature of volunteering, and from that research-based starting point the board asked how we could use what was learned to realign various bodies of the organization, including the representative assembly.

Out of this research AOTA also learned that members were more interested in being better practitioners than the "bureaucratic stuff, including governance." So the recommendations were tailored to make it easier and more fulfilling for members to participate.

The ad-hoc committee produced a set of "recommendations for enhancing association participation," including creating a number of new committees and systems for improving membership volunteer and leadership development. These were incorporated into the governance restructuring plan. But the

(continued)

(*continued*)

plan was not accepted. Somers recounted the change agents' first defeat:

> Our president at the time initiated the review and new proposed structure with the full support of the board. Unfortunately, the recommendations were rejected in the Assembly by a margin of four or five votes. And our president got beat up pretty good. We knew going in that it was going to be challenging. A third of the group were old-timers bound and determined not to change. Nonetheless, the debate did underscore that a large segment was willing to consider change if it was incremental and approached in stages.

Strategy: Recognize the Needs of Change Opponents

Somers and Bluhm observed that resistance to these changes was somewhat about lack of context and fear over the outcomes. Volunteers' perspectives may be limited to their own responsibilities (e.g., committees) and to how the change affects what they know and hold dear, rather than what is best for the association overall.

A huge piece of the lesson for the AOTA board was the level of pushback that came from people uncomfortable that the board was driving this change. According to Bluhm:

> It was incredibly painful. Some elements of the representative assembly and the membership saw "conspiracy" and thought the board was trying to hijack the organization.

Strategy: Persistence and Patience

But the board did not give up. Capitalizing on the sentiment of those willing to consider incremental change, the assembly in 2010 approved the creation of a second ad-hoc committee with the same charge. They changed the composition to include more representation from the assembly. Somers recalled what happened next:

> The second ad-hoc committee came to essentially the same recommendations. After taking this extra time and being part of the process, the current leaders started to understand and embrace the proposed changes. People who were not a part of the process could not make that leap—it was a bridge too far. I do believe if we could have taken the entire representative assembly through the second ad-hoc committee process, it would have been a slam-dunk.

But although the second ad-hoc committee came to the same recommendations, the full representative assembly again rejected the proposal by a similar margin. And then a big external event occurred that forced the change. The new District of Columbia Nonprofit Corporation Act (Title 29 of the D.C. Code—Business Organizations Code) took effect January 1, 2012. In the code, Section 29-406.01(b) provided:

> Except as otherwise provided in § 29-406.12, all corporate powers shall be exercised by or under the authority of the board of directors of the nonprofit corporation, and the activities and affairs of the corporation shall be managed by or under the directors, and subject to the oversight, of the board of directors.

(continued)

(*continued*)

Somers observed:

This of course clarified the role of the board and enabled us to address the ambiguity and overlap that existed in our old bylaws between responsibilities of the board and the representative assembly. Also, the new statute provided for the creation of "designated bodies of the board" to delegate clearly circum-scribed board responsibilities. This provision allowed us to continue maintaining an assembly, which was important, albeit with much more clearly drawn authority, in our case to address professional policies and standards.

This change required a major revision of the bylaws to remove the ambiguity over organizational authority and provide clarity in roles and responsibilities. The assembly previously had some responsibility over budget and financial policies. Under the new D.C. law, that had to go.

Strategy: Educate Members to Help Them Adapt to New Policies

Today the representative assembly is a designated body of the board responsible explicitly for professional standards and policies. To encourage understanding and buy-in for the bylaws' changes, AOTA held webinars and circulated the bylaws for comment both to the members of the representative assembly and the general membership. Somers recalled:

We did as much member education as any organization can possibly do. Still, when we got to our annual business meeting at the 2013 conference, there was still some vocal opposition. There was always a subset of membership that viewed this as a board power-grab rather than a change required by law. Yet in the spring of 2013, the bylaws were finally approved.

Today, according to Somers, AOTA's board is forward-looking and proactive:

> A new cohort of leaders are coming in and learning. The assembly is working on leadership development within its ranks, and on being more proactive on professional issues; it's a function of a leadership learning curve. There is no more wearing of multiple hats or confusion about fiduciary responsibilities versus perceived responsibilities to constituencies. There remains more for us to do—it's an evolutionary process. But overall, we have achieved our goals.

Strategy: Proactive Volunteer Recruitment and Development

The board of directors and, more informally, Somers and the senior staff can now focus on informal candidate identification and recruitment to bring in volunteers:

> The organization traditionally was somewhat laissez-faire about candidate vetting. We are now more proactive. We have had a great pipeline of outstanding presidents over the past 10 years, with a large group of talent in the queue. We work to provide a more professional orientation process with incoming board members and those in other volunteer positions so they understand their fiduciary responsibilities. I began taking our new president and vice president to the two ASAE symposia for executive and board leaders. We now conduct an annual board self-assessment process to keep on track. We are just more mindful about tending the board development "garden."
>
> And we have strengthened our financial status. This helps the boardroom dynamic immensely, allowing [directors] to be strategic and not worry about operations or financial stability. We have disaster plans in place and we have what-if conversations with the board

We are more mindful about tending the board development "garden."

(continued)

(continued)

each winter meeting about things that could go off the track. I'm a strong believer in having conversations about trends and the potential impacts of those trends. "No surprises" is Rule Number One. I want them to be aware of what's going on in the external environment that could have an impact on our operations.

Today the board is clearly focused on governing. The AOTA board has three face-to-face meetings a year and holds conference calls as needed. An officers' call every month (with minutes sent to the full board), a board listserv, and a monthly CEO report ensure continuity in communication. And today, as Somers puts it, the board operates under one simple rule: "No surprises."

3 | Catalysts and Watersheds

You never want a serious crisis to go to waste.
— Rahm Emanuel, Mayor, City of Chicago

Julia Hamm is president and CEO of the Solar Electric Power Association. Until 2003, SEPA had been run by a management services company. Hamm came on board as the first actual employee in 2004. She recalls the board she inherited:

There were no continuing programs and no infrastructure; we had to build from the ground up. We had a very hands-on operating board (midlevel managers from the companies within our membership), and we largely needed them to be active in this way.

But around 2008, we skyrocketed. The industry was changing and our organization gained prominence because of what was happening with the growing need for changes in the world's energy resources. Solar was no longer an afterthought. We grew very quickly, from one to twenty employees, from a hundred to a thousand members, from a budget of $300,000 to $6 million. It became clear to me that we no longer needed the board to be involved in day-to-day operations.

As will be shown in SEPA's case, described in full at the end of this chapter, transformational or other types of change often occur through what Lynn Isabella (1993, p. 18) describes as "trigger events." These are catalyzing events that require a full organizational reaction and may precipitate new behaviors and mindsets on the part of leadership.

Their magnitude and potential for organizational [and] personal impact set in motion a series of mental shifts as individuals strive to understand and redefine the situation. By their very nature [trigger events] unbalance established routines and evoke conscious thought on the part of organizational members. . . . In short, trigger events bring people's mindsets into the arena of change.

Trigger events describe situations that an organization may not be able to address through pre-established organizational routines. And in the case of the stories in this book, the trigger events caused board members and staff to realize that their organization could not respond without a better board. In the general management literature, trigger events may include mergers, relocations, new leadership, reorganizations, downsizings, rapid growth, new strategic directions, or unanticipated crises (Isabella 1993). In the following section, we describe the patterns of events that triggered *governance* change in organizations studied for this book.

Concepts and Application

Many Windows of Opportunity

Chicago Mayor Rahm Emanuel's quote at the beginning of this chapter closely mirrors what we heard from some of our interviewees.

Wylecia Wiggs Harris, COO of the American Nurses Association, also observed, "Don't waste a crisis." The point illustrates two important ideas: First, organizational leaders must recognize that any new event—whether a crisis or a grand success—may offer a window of opportunity for a new outlook on governance. Some events challenge an organization's very survival. We heard stories of lawsuits, deaths, and other serious crises. These events could be quite traumatic, as our stories will relate.

Other times, there was no crisis at all, just opportunity. As David Harvey of the Society of Estate and Trust Practitioners told us:

> We were lucky we were not in a crisis situation. We had recognized the need for change before change was desperately needed. It's harder to enact change when it's forced upon you.

Some catalyzing events could be described as a gentle nudge—a simple question about term limits or board member recruitment that started a generative conversation about improving the board. Tracie Kenyon of the Montana Credit Union Network recalled:

> Members were already having a conversation about "redistricting." I said, "Don't you really mean *governing*?" But not all of our board members felt this way. I told them there are two sacred cows in associations, the dues structure and the governance structure, and we need to talk about them both every year. We can't just leave the elephant sitting in the room until the elephant is dead. So we started to have the conversation. The dues conversation happened first, in my first year of employment. That was the low-hanging fruit—easier to talk about, so that's where we started. It helped to foster the culture we needed for governance change later.

What made the outcome successful for the people behind these stories was the will to seize opportunity. Shannon Carter, CAE, of the Competency & Credentialing Institute (CCI) recalls:

> When I arrived CCI was in a turnaround situation. Not financially—they were solvent—but they needed to move to a more effective

model of governance for this organization's life cycle. It was an outgrowth of some painful board–staff relationships. The board recognized that change was needed.

Many Starting Points

The second idea is that governance change does not share a single starting point. An analysis of the initial catalyzing events for the board changes we studied identified two major sources, which we have termed "insider action" and "unexpected events," displayed in Table 3.1. We also display both possible negative outcomes as they

Table 3.1 Starting Points for Governance Change

Catalyzing Events	Examples	Possible Negative Outcomes	Strategies for Success
Insider action	Board initiates change.	Staff resistance to new ideas.	Communication. Invest in professional staff development.
	Current CEO initiates change.	Board resistance to new ideas.	Board education. Scout for new board members as change agents.
	Board hires CEO as change agent.	Membership or section resistance.	Transparent and inclusive change process.
Unexpected events/ shocks to the system	Regulatory level: Change to state nonprofit law forces bylaws change.	Board caught by surprise. Section resistance if forced to change bylaws to conform	Advance awareness of legislative trends and of Model Nonprofit Corporation Act.

Table 3.1 (*continued*)

Catalyzing Events	Examples	Possible Negative Outcomes	Strategies for Success
		with national board. Member resistance to sudden end to shared governance.	
	Organizational level: Fiscal crisis, rapid growth, rapid decline, scandal, merger, turnover, new accreditation requirements.	Challenges of dealing with a crisis while addressing governance change.	Clearly defined roles and responsibilities for crisis management (i.e., organizational spokesperson, common messaging). Developing a two-track system for dealing with crisis and dealing with change.
	Board level: Major policy disagreement, lawsuit.	Board factions, dissension.	Active communication; use of outside facilitation.
	Staff level: CEO departure, health crisis.	Board or other staff respond to fill the "leadership vacuum"; get in the weeds; power grabs; confusion.	Predetermined Emergency Succession Plan in place that gets activated.

were described to us and strategies for success suggested by the association leaders we interviewed.

Insider Action

Practically speaking, all governance change begins via insider action, since a board is legally responsible for changing its own structure. Our research discovered two kinds of change agents operating from within: executive staff already employed within the organization, who initiated action, or board members who did so. As Table 3.1 reflects, what these organizations experienced and what strategies they used to guarantee success varied as well. We briefly list here and will discuss in more detail in Chapters 5 through 7 the suggested strategies for board-led, staff-led, and jointly led governance change.

Here are two comments we heard in cases where association executive directors served as the change agents:

1. "When I joined them 12 years ago, they were in the middle of a significant financial crisis. Actually, the upside of it meant that they were willing to listen to me because there were some emergency measures that had to be taken."
2. "When I was hired, the board was comprised of two factions. They were almost at war. No trust, little communication. They were losing money, were not following policies and procedures, and it was somewhat political. With work the result was a more knowledgeable, visionary board. Infighting stopped. More open communication. Better overall relationships across the board. Everyone developed trust and confidence."

However, as our analysis found, the most common trigger events came from the board members themselves, particularly when new members brought knowledge about good governance with them:

"Several board members ran on a change ticket."

"We had a couple of board members who knew there was a different way to do things because they had prior governance experience."
"The board decided to do a strategic planning session that had previously been run and supported by the staff. This led to a larger level of engagement."

In some instances, boards recognized the need for change and hired their next CEO as a change agent. Study participants observed:

"The board realized they could not get out of the weeds until they hired somebody to take care of the weeds for them."
"Our evolution started with the commitment to hire the first association professional."

Sometimes, the first inside person to recognize a need for change was the board's presiding officer. We heard the following accounts from executive directors:

"The chair told me he was tired of sitting around and seeing the board not doing anything."
"I wasn't looking for something new for my sake. Things were going well. And an executive director needs to deliver the means and not the ends. So for the president to say, 'Let's look at this,' was significant. It was so great for somebody else to pose it."

Unexpected Events

Organization leaders also recounted many examples of unplanned change that began as a result of an external shock to the system, crisis, or other unplanned event. These events caused board members and staff to recognize the need or opportunity and galvanize the organization into action (for observations on how such events change perceptions, see our section on Malcolm Gladwell's "tipping points" in Chapter 4). Our analysis of these stories suggests four levels of external influence on the governance system: regulatory-, organizational-, board-, or staff-level events or crises.

At the regulatory level, we have already heard one story of an association, AOTA, that took advantage of a change in public law to restructure its board. AOTA's story is interesting in that its leaders were already involved in a deep, somewhat painful, but also generative discussion with members about effective association leadership. Since they could not put off the need to revise bylaws to conform to public laws, the new nonprofit incorporation law served as a useful tipping point toward governance change that was already underway.

At the organizational level, fiscal crises, rapid growth, scandals, and new accreditation requirements caused a variety of responses by association boards. In some instances, having any change thrust upon the entire organization generally fostered a healthier outlook among board members about governance change specifically. Dorothy Mitstifer, executive director of Kappa Omicron Nu, described how a merger between two associations caused her board to easily accept the need for governance restructuring: "After the merger it wasn't strange to look at something new."

At other associations, leaders pointed out that major organizational events required their board members to evolve to be more effective during the transition. In the words of S. Joe DeHaven of the Indiana Bankers Association: "We *had* to have good board leadership during that change. Every aspect of the merger had to be battled out."

At the board level, dissension and bad internal politics can force the board to hold a mirror to itself. But we did not hear many stories about entirely dysfunctional boards, and that fact suggests that healthy governance change is usually preemptive and occurs before an association's board has reached the point of failure.

And while a board may initially feel a need for some kind of change, sometimes it takes a new CEO to clearly articulate that change is not just needed but imperative. As will be shown in the case of the Association for Corporate Growth at the end of this chapter, board chair Chuck Morton noted: "When [our new CEO] came, all of our organization's records were in the trunk in a staff member's car. We were a mess."

Finally, at the staff level, association boards may be forced to confront change—or may find new opportunities—when a longtime executive director departs. Our interviews reflected two circumstances where unexpected staff changes impelled governance change. In some cases, longtime (sometimes founding) executive directors had *prevented* change from happening. In other cases, longtime executive directors clearly saw the opportunity for change and sometimes even facilitated governance change in the course of their departure. In both cases, a CEO's retirement or passing required the board to step up and accept its responsibilities. Dennis Simmons, AAP, recently retired CEO of the Southwestern Automated Clearing House Association, told us:

> I've been with the association for almost 18 years. I told my board that someday I would like to retire! I was the catalyst but when the light bulb went on, the board got over its denial that I was leaving. One of our board members was going through a similar process herself and she became the driver for succession planning.

Summary

These paths to governance change reveal many starting points and suggest organizations can take advantage of many windows of opportunity to achieve governance change. This diversity in unfolding events has its own contradictions and dynamic tensions. In some associations, change was bound to happen and insiders simply recognized and facilitated the opportunity to grow, whereas in others, someone forced change upon an unwilling organization or

In some associations, change was bound to happen and insiders simply recognized and facilitated the opportunity to grow, while in others, someone forced change upon an unwilling organization or board.

Table 3.2   Catalyzing Events in Governance Change: Three Major Dimensions

1. Change that was bound to happen versus change that was forced
2. Need-driven change versus resource-driven change
3. Staff-inspired change versus board-inspired change

board. In some cases, change was brought on by a budget crisis or other need, but in others the evolution of the board was supported by healthy growth and new resources. Some change was staff-driven; other change was board-inspired (Table 3.2).

The stories we heard do suggest that each dimension of these catalyzing events has its own particular challenges. For example, need-driven board change involved some painful transitional periods for boards and staff dealing with the stress of financial problems. But change agents who initiated a board restructuring when the organization was healthy struggled with other challenges, mostly of the "why fix what isn't broken?" kind. Understanding board change from this multidimensional perspective also brings home the point that regardless of who starts the ball rolling, everyone will need to be involved in the outcome. The following two cases—Solar Electric Power Association and Association for Corporate Growth—illustrate how associations leveraged opportunities for board change by taking advantage of growth.

Using Growth to Make the Case for Governance Change

Case: Solar Electric Power Association

 Solar power is rapidly gaining credibility in the utility industry, and the young Solar Electric Power Association understood that greater effectiveness and growth was contingent upon having greater representation from the C-Suite on its board.

Learn how their first CEO framed an effective "call to arms" to restructure the board and its membership, transformed the culture of the board to emphasize strategic leadership, and retained the goodwill of former board members along the way.

SEPA is an "educational nonprofit organization dedicated to helping utilities integrate solar energy into their portfolio" (www.solarelectricpower.org/about-sepa.aspx; Figure 3.1). SEPA's membership comprises more than 900 electric utilities, solar companies, and other organizations with an interest in solar electricity. Founded in 1992, SEPA describes itself as "the go-to resource for unbiased solar intelligence and collaborative dialogue between utilities and the solar industry."

Challenge: Outgrowing an Operational Board

As President and CEO Julia Hamm recounted in the passage at the beginning of this chapter, SEPA's explosive growth to a fully staffed organization meant that its operational governance model was no longer needed. The future of SEPA required a different kind of board.

David Rubin, a Pacific Gas & Electric employee and former board chair, was one of the individuals for whom the light bulb went on:

I started on the board in 2005, and we were more engaged in the details rather than looking far forward and charting a direction for the organization. It was where solar resided in the utility industry at that point in time. Most of the people who were into solar were midlevel engineers then.

(continued)

(continued)

Challenge: Need for Change Not Recognized

Hamm began to plant the seeds for a governance change by first building up her social capital with more senior-level people within SEPA's member companies. But there were challenges:

> There were many people who had been on the board for a very long time. They were very proud of the role they played on the board and in the organization. This also gave them prominence within their own company. When I first started the conversation, it was heard but not embraced.

From the boardroom, Rubin recalled:

> Part of the difficulty of executing some of the changes has been that it's a great organization to be a board member of. A lot of us enjoy the work, the stature of the position. But we realized we needed a much more visionary organization.

Strategy: Make the Case for Change

Hamm developed a confidential SEPA Governance white paper (below, in edited and abbreviated form) to describe how the maturation of the nonprofit offered opportunities that depended in turn on a different kind of board member:

> Every Board is expected to evolve as an organization matures. A maturing organization demands that a Board meets its needs at any point in time.

Historically SEPA relied on its Board of Directors to provide basic support, including operational guidance, insight into the day-to-day issues faced by the membership, and input on member programs and services. However, SEPA has evolved substantially over the past few years with substantial operational expertise on staff and a strong track record.

SEPA is discovering, at this stage of its development, that its needs of the Board are changing and with those changes comes the realization that the Board as currently constructed may not optimally contribute what is currently most needed. Today, the greatest value the Board can offer SEPA is providing **leadership, guidance, and vision**, enhancing and improving its **image and stature** within the utility/energy industry, while opening doors to **external funding** opportunities.

Leadership, Guidance, and Vision—The landscape for electric utilities is anticipated to change substantially in the coming years. . . . Business models will be shifting, the role of policy will be changing, and new partnership models will arise. The SEPA Board today requires individuals who can share perspectives on issues and solutions related to next-generation electric utility business models, looking beyond the "renewable energy silo." Future SEPA Board Directors will be comfortable providing guidance and vision to promote and position SEPA as the thought leader for participating utilities (and solar companies) creating win-win solutions. Managing to the "cutting edge" is the goal, and leadership coming from the Board of Directors will help get us there faster.

Image and Stature—SEPA has grown its image and stature with high-level energy industry executives substantially over the past 3 to 4 years. . . . Utility executives across the country promote their company's place in SEPA's Top 10 Awards. To build on this momentum, SEPA's Board Directors should be positioned to use their connections and stature to promote SEPA into opportunities to further enhance its brand awareness, including participation in executive meetings/forums,

(continued)

(*continued*)

contributing to news stories in industry publications, and creating speaking opportunities at high-profile energy industry events.

External Funding—SEPA is working to diversify its revenue. . . . SEPA's Board members should be well positioned to identify new funding and business opportunities for the organization, and should be prepared to open doors to those opportunities. . . . SEPA Board members should have access to and the ear of decision makers at the top of their organization, and must be able and willing to position SEPA as an entity uniquely suited to help utilities with increasingly important challenges and opportunities involving solar energy.

Opportunity—If the premise is correct, and that to grow SEPA requires new leadership from a new class of Board member, is SEPA ready or able to recruit to a level desired or required?

Strategy: Bring Evidence

After making the case for a new governance model, Hamm had to show evidence that the "Opportunity" question posed above was achievable. Hamm and board members who had served on the board's nominating committee documented examples of senior utility executives who had previously put themselves forward for consideration for the SEPA board but were unsuccessful at gaining election. It was an eye-opening moment:

We found that the midlevel people who had been on our nominating committee in past years were thinking these folks were too high level and wouldn't really be able to commit the time necessary to serve. It was a "holy-moly" moment when we went back to our list of people who had volunteered and failed to make the cut and realized how many were the high-level people we now needed.

The SEPA Governance white paper continued to note:

The question remains as to what SEPA will make of [this opportunity to recruit a different kind of board member] while conserving the value of those currently serving. The answer may be in restructuring the organization to retain the benefits and contributions of existing Board members, while allowing the Board itself to breathe, if not grow into a higher-level body that may provide the leadership, guidance, and vision that the organization demands today.

Continued Engagement Opportunities—The composition of SEPA's Board today is a mix of types of individuals, some who fit the "old" mold and others the "new" mold. Those who fit the old mold have a very important ongoing role to play within the organization. It is critical to develop a structure that allows them to get the continued value out of their engagement with SEPA and allows SEPA to continue to benefit from their commitment to the organization.

These objectives can be accomplished with the formation of standing committees that allow individuals with common interests to engage on a regular basis and provide input and guidance to SEPA staff on programs and services of relevance to their own interests. Participation on these committees could be by appointment of the board . . . or open to all members. . . . This type of committee structure would also create additional opportunities for engagement between more of our utility and solar industry members.

(continued)

(*continued*)

Hamm describes the process of accepting this new model as an *evolution*:

Light bulbs went on at different times with different board members, the recognition that "I may not be the right person on this board; maybe my boss or boss's boss should be on this board." This led to the [governance] transformation.

Strategy: Creating a Process for Change

Hamm describes how careful meeting management supported the process of change:

I was able to use selective board members to move the process along and we were fortunate to use Bruce Lesley from BoardSource as an independent third-party expert to initially pose the tough questions about potential changes in board composition and governance. It wasn't like I had a roadmap, but looking back I see that it was very well orchestrated.

Table 3.3 is Bruce Lesley's abbreviated agenda for a crucial SEPA board meeting in April 2013.

Table 3.3   Board of Directors Meeting: Portland, OR

8:30 Call to Order, Welcome, and Self-Introductions: David Rubin, Chair

8:40 A Vision for the Future: Julia Hamm, President and CEO

9:00 How are we progressing with our current Strategic Direction? Review of Governance Responsibilities: Bruce Lesley, facilitator

9:30 What does it mean to govern in the fiduciary, strategic, and resource development modes?

What is an exceptional board's role in strategic planning?

Review and discuss: Mission facilitator; all

What does the following mission statement mean to us?

> SEPA is an educational nonprofit organization dedicated to helping utilities integrate solar energy into their portfolio for the benefit of the utility, its customers, and the public good.

What are the guiding principles or beliefs that should drive decision making based on this mission statement?

6. What are the most significant *external* measures of success in support of our mission, not the internal performance of the association or CEO?

11:45 Lunch and meetings

1:15

7. Review and discuss select strategies and issues: Facilitator; all

What are the major activities or measures to ensure success?

What is an exceptional board's role in each strategic area of emphasis, if any?

7.1. How can the board of directors help SEPA with its revenue diversification strategies and efforts to broaden its value proposition?

7.2. Under what circumstances and within what guidelines should SEPA take a position on an issue?

7.3. Under what circumstances and within what guidelines should SEPA expand its reach or scope?

(continued)

Table 3.3 *(continued)*

7.4. Within which opportunities and under what circumstances or guidelines should SEPA enter into partnerships with other nonprofits? How should these be approached?

7.5. What approaches should SEPA consider to provide more opportunities for member engagement? How can we make these opportunities prestigious?

7.6. What are your broad policy thoughts on a "SEPA designation program" that recognizes utilities for achieving set solar milestones?

7.7. How can SEPA most effectively facilitate common standards and best practices among utilities and solar companies? On which critical issues should these efforts focus?

7.8. Are there any other major activities/measures on the current Strategic Focus Areas listed in the following? How should the board support these efforts?

7.8.1. Serve as a thought leader in the area of utility use and integration of solar.

7.8.2. Provide information, analysis, and relationships that result in increased utility industry knowledge on the subject of solar technologies, programs, and policies.

7.8.3. Communicate to the renewable energy industry, media, and general public the important role utilities play in increasing the amount of solar energy in the national energy portfolio.

3:15

8. Review and discuss selected Board Structure: Facilitator; all

8.1. Based on the previous discussions, what should board members be doing between board or committee meetings to help advance SEPA's strategies and mission?

8.2. How can we improve the cultivation and recruiting of the right leaders (i.e., maintaining or raising our leadership level)?

8.3. Do we have any other ideas for improving the board's effectiveness (e.g., size, term limits, officers, meetings, board committees, technology support)?

4:00

9. Next steps: Chair, president, facilitator

What is the process to move forward from these discussions?

How will this feedback be used to define a new strategic direction?

Source: Solar Electric Power Association.

Strategy: Practice a New Way of Leading

Rubin observed how the planned changes challenged board members to think differently not only about their roles, but also about their own seats on the board:

> The changes occurred over an extended period of time. First, we as board members got better at the game in terms of stepping away from the details. Then we also looked in the mirror and realized the board members present during this change didn't necessarily carry the same skills that would be necessary to see us into the future. It wasn't until 2012 that my light bulb finished switching on—when I also realized that I needed to get somebody at a higher level in my company to put their hat in the ring and take on a leadership position at SEPA.

Strategy: Put Change Agents on Nominating Committee

> Hamm relates that SEPA took advantage of natural attrition allowed under their bylaws: If a seat became vacant before a term was up, the board chair could nominate someone to fill the seat. Hamm worked with David Rubin as chair to use those opportunities to appoint people to the board who fit the mold of the future board they envisioned. The first people who fit well were asked to sit on the nominating committee to find more nominees like them. And because the transition plan was transparent, the nominating committee helped the change along.

Strategy: Use Early Wins to Maintain Momentum

Once the transitions in board composition were well under way, Hamm, Rubin, and others on the board became

(continued)

(*continued*)

convinced that additional improvements were necessary. According to Hamm:

> Late last year I proposed to the board that we form a governance committee. We are now doing a total governance overhaul. It will culminate in a new set of bylaws.
>
> The impetus for having a governance committee was really because for a long time I believed we needed term limits. Over the past eight years I tried to raise the issue many times but coming from me it was not going over well. In order to be successful, it had to come from the board itself. And from a process standpoint, it wasn't going to happen at the board meetings. It had to come from a governance committee. I started researching what governance committees do and then started realizing there were all kinds of other governance changes we should be considering.

So SEPA board members also created a board officer succession plan, updated officer job descriptions, and changed officer elections processes to identify candidates and their interest in serving in advance. They assessed all standing board committees through the lens of their strategic plan. Standing board committee chairs are now elected by the full board rather than selected by each committee, and committees are populated through executive committee appointment with primary consideration for the needs of the organization rather than individual preferences. Committee chairs joined officers on the executive committee. Term limits for board seats were added, bylaws were streamlined to include only what is required by law, and a board policy manual addressed the additional specifics of governance formerly included in the bylaws. Board meetings added a consent agenda to free up time.

Here is how Hamm assesses SEPA's current situation:

> We are about 60 percent of the way there in terms of having the right people on the board, and now the transition is accelerating. We are continuing to strengthen the board committee structure for

more empowerment—to use board committees to do the work so the board can focus on strategic conversations when it meets.

Strategy: Be Willing to Compromise

When asked about the lessons learned and the advice she would offer other associations, Hamm laughed:

Ask us again in a year. So far we've avoided hurt feelings. The board has made accommodations to those members who would be most vocal. In our conversations early on with the governance committee, most people felt that two three-year terms felt like a good place. But then they decided we should make it three terms with a grandfathering provision for long-serving members. I didn't think that was in our best organizational interests, but I was willing to let go. It was a compromise.

Strategy: Incremental Change

One thing I can't really say was right or wrong, good or bad, was how we instituted the changes. We have spread out governance changes over the course of 12 months. There is something to be said for that. Overall we have been more successful because we fed bits of this to the board over time, a smaller pill to swallow for some. But it's also a longer, more drawn-out process, and some board members wish we could do it quicker and rip the Band-Aid off all at once. A year from now maybe I'll be able to look back and say which way would have been best.

Rubin joined in:

I can't say either whether an incremental approach or a Band-Aid rip-off is better, but I do think we could have started sooner. We didn't start the process as quickly as we could have.

(continued)

(*continued*)

Hamm agreed:

Yes, I wish we could have started the process sooner. But I also wish I had started intentionally to build the pipeline of people I wanted on the board sooner. I waited for the board to be ready before I started building relationships. I now wish I had already developed a deeper pool of people to draw from.

"Grow or Die" for Governance Change

Case: Association for Corporate Growth

When Gary LaBranche was hired as CEO of the Association for Corporate Growth, he wasn't even recognized by many of the autonomous chapters. Learn how he took advantage of the Recession to build a professional staff, earn the board's and chapters' trust, and allow an operational board to focus on where it was needed strategically—serving members, strengthening chapter services, and building an accountable, integrated, and truly global association.

The Association for Corporate Growth (ACG) provides a global community for mergers and acquisitions and corporate growth professionals, with 56 chapters in North America, South America, Asia, and Europe. Founded in 1954, ACG has grown to more than 14,500 members from private equity firms, lenders, and professional service firms that focus on midmarket companies (www.acg.org/global/about/).

ACG developed as a chapter-centered association with strong local chapter autonomy. The association focused on helping members to do business with other members through face-to-face networking. The global association was deliberately kept very weak, focusing on starting new chapters and running the annual meeting. The global association was managed by part-time staff provided by a small association management company. The 30-member board met three to four times a year. ACG's mission was stated in a 56-word paragraph, which made it difficult to articulate a clear value proposition to members.

Challenge: Weak Strategic Orientation

Gary A. LaBranche, FASAE, CAE, now serves as ACG's president and CEO. LaBranche noted that many described the board he inherited as an elite, closed club. The board had only recently adopted firm term limits; previously, people served on the board for as long as 15 years:

> Before I came, the board was operationally focused. It was probably not a bad way to go when the association was small, but things were different by the 1990s. For example, the bylaws were written to forbid political advocacy, even though we are a (c)6. And the organization needed to be thinking about advocacy.

Challenge: Members Demand More Than Board Can Deliver

The world was changing, member needs were changing, but the organization was not yet positioned to lead strategically. LaBranche recalled:

(continued)

(continued)

The changes really began with growth. In the early 1990s, the association started to grow, mostly because of positive regulatory changes, and our membership base began to grow exponentially. The board and small staff were overwhelmed by the growth. The chapter leaders also realized they needed more services from the global board and office staff.

In 1995, there began a civil war in ACG. Some of the bigger chapters started to rebel and demand better services from ACG. They threatened to quit and go solo.

But forward-looking leaders got on the board with a plan to create a more strategic association that could support its chapters. By mid-2000, with a board composed of half old guard and half new guard, they agreed to hire the first full-time CEO and create an in-house staff. The newer leaders understood they could not have a truly strategic board until they had a professional staff. As LaBranche observed:

You can't get out of the weeds until you have hired somebody to take care of the weeds for you.

A new CEO was hired in late 2005. Back-office operations and other services were shifted from the long-serving AMC to a new association management company, SmithBucklin. But LaBranche recalls that the board still had a lot of operational power:

Board members were still choosing napkin colors for the annual meeting. Board members independently made agreements and committed the organization on pet projects. Bad decisions were made.

And while the first CEO made some strides, he struggled with chapter relations and left in late 2007.

Strategy: Build Impetus for Change

By 2008, a new generation of board members was in place, with a vision to create a true strategic board. That's when LaBranche arrived:

I came on as CEO in September 2008. It was terrible timing with the financial meltdown. But the challenges imposed by the recession presented an opportunity to make real change occur. We were aligned and focused, but we recognized that we had to prove our worth to and gain the trust of the chapters and members.

Strategy: Build Internal Capacity for Change

LaBranche notes that ACG benefited from having SmithBucklin provide the back-office operations before he arrived, especially during a period of rapid growth. But his job was to build an in-house team, to better control ACG's destiny and achieve economies of scale. He on-boarded some SmithBucklin staff for critical continuity, achieving full operational independence in fall 2013.

Strategy: Build Board's Trust in Staff

LaBranche recalls that his next challenge was to get the board to trust the staff, so that the board would feel comfortable letting go

(continued)

(*continued*)

of operational decisions. However, despite the board's articulated ambitions, some things took a while:

> For example, it took two years for me to gain authority to manage the annual meeting—a board member chaired the meeting and maintained authority over budget and many planning decisions. Early on, I sometimes wasn't even invited to attend planning meetings. So I insisted on additional authority, noting that they could hardly hold me accountable for the overall budget if I did not have control of our $4 million convention. They agreed, but with careful oversight from the finance committee, a condition that was dropped after a year. This step, along with new services made possible by bringing the staff in-house, generated many positive outcomes, most notably with chapters. Patience, competency, and a service culture was our strategy. The result is the strong level of trust that the board and chapter leaders now have in the professional staff.

Charles (Chuck) J. Morton, Jr., Esq., partner of Venable, LLC, had been a member of ACG for a long time. He initially became involved through a chapter, becoming board chair in 2012. He recalls:

> Our board had to see that staff could do it, or they would have reverted back to an operational role. We hired people aspirationally, in positions that we knew would grow. We gave the change leaders on the board the ability to stand up in front of their peers and say, "Look, we don't have to do such-and-such anymore; the staff can do it for us better."

Challenge: Weak Chapter Trust in the National Board

Morton also described a key challenge they encountered as a weak national board:

For most of our members, the chapter experience is how they define ACG. Today, individual ACG chapters are found around the world on four continents, but back in 2000 there was no way to ensure continuity. It was a loose confederation with no mechanism for knitting the chapters together. Chapters were using our brand without Global ACG (the international association) having any meaningful way to coordinate activity for the good of the whole. Some of them were very powerful economically and were not necessarily reflecting the best practices of governance or organizational development—they had grown organically and in some cases awkwardly. Yet when Gary came, all of our organization's records were in the trunk in a key staff member's car. We were a mess.

But we had something special. We serve an industry that relies upon the ability to build community. We had a diversity of professional expertise in a part of the economy that is very robust, and people who were doing well financially. We were succeeding in spite of ourselves.

Strategy: Use Staff Turnover as an Opportunity

From Chuck Morton's perspective, the difficult experience with ACG's short-lived first CEO also offered an opportunity to manage chapter relations more effectively:

(*continued*)

(continued)

It helped us to identify the challenges we were facing. And it gave us the opportunity to bring in a seasoned association management professional who understood the kinds of challenges that face associations all the time. Through that clarity of vision, Gary, supported by our board, was able in a strategic way to create links between our chapters. He helped us institute chapter affiliation agreements; guidelines governing the use of our logo and brand; opportunities to clearly define "the ACG experience." And in those instances where chapters had gone somewhat rogue he gave us an ability to create mechanisms for accountability within the multi-chapter network. When we look back 20 years from now, *that* accomplishment, which was achieved without a lot of controversy, will be seen as pivotal.

Strategy: Take Advantage of Association's Culture

Morton observed:

One of the nice things about our community is that we are dealmakers. Members and chapters got the fact that if we are going to be a thing, we had to have some rules to keep the thing together—some way, some framework that defines something and gives us strength. In the absence of that we would be nothing.

Strategy: Use Evidence of Value to Create Trust in the Change

ACG got some people behind the new model quickly, aiming for the low-hanging fruit. But some members took more persuading. Morton described the board's strategy with chapters:

We said, "If you wish to remain a chapter, you need to be on our page." Our global staff was consistently providing more support and services to the chapters than ever before. Global ACG was creating value, which helped to create a lot more trust. The chapters agreed to abide by our bylaws, which helped to frame a meaningful infrastructure.

One of the nice things about our community is that we are deal makers. They got the fact that if we are going to be a thing, we had to have some rules to keep the thing together.

LaBranche notes: "Part of it was positioning ACG as a competent culture, and asking how we could better serve the chapters."

Morton added:

We have been through a cycle of modeling behavior for the chapters. Global ACG has been consistently finding ways to help the chapters. And because of the connection we have been able to provide, chapters do innovative programming, learn from each other, and there is a better sharing of resources. Now there is a sense that we are all in this together, a fundamental change in how we function.

The role of the board changed dramatically. We went from a board that was action oriented to a board focused on governance, creating a strategic plan, and holding a great staff accountable. When we made that change, we were able to accomplish remarkable things.

The role of the board changed dramatically. We went from a board that was an action-oriented board to a board focused on governance, creating a strategic plan, and holding a great staff accountable. When we made that change, we were able to accomplish remarkable things.

(continued)

(*continued*)

Strategy: Invest in Strategic Planning

ACG developed a strategic plan that emphasized facilitating member business relationships and supporting members technologically. In addition, the plan called for a ramp-up in services to chapters, chapter leaders, and chapter executives. Morton notes its importance:

> Our strategic planning process was essential. We used Harrison Coerver and Associates for the strategic planning process. It was grounded in reality but allowed us to have a vision to be at a better, higher place. For the first time in the organization's history we articulated a clear, distinct, and aspirational mission and vision. We have our strategic plan on our board business cards now.

Outcomes

LaBranche looked back on six years as CEO:

> My board right now is about as strategic as I could hope for. So the change has happened. It took about six years—2007 to 2013. We have 27 board members now. We do a board training and orientation every year. The ASAE-sponsored CEO-board training is required for senior leaders. Just the process of getting them together for a couple of days talking about things helps to create alignment.
>
> We've built a culture and support system that keeps our leaders focused on policy and strategy. We enforce focus on mission and goals with board members; we use external strategic consultants for forecasting; board members are asked to bring

outside data and information to help us keep an external perspective. The board agenda is now organized in three parts: leadership (foresight), stewardship (oversight), membership (insight).

We also have built-in continuity at the leadership level. In the "Office of the Chair," we have the current board chair, the chair-elect (elected as the vice chair), and the immediate past chair. They are the "carriers of the culture of the organization" and stewards of the strategic plan. This group keeps both the board and me appropriately focused. The strategic plan is the blueprint we try to follow. It helps the ACG to have agility, nimbleness, and adaptability while not swinging so far away from its goals because of the "it's my year" mentality. I bounce things off them all the time. We talk on a regular basis. Their charge is to "sustain a relentless focus on the strategic plan." They maintain the culture we want.

Morton and LaBranche credit timing, luck, persistence, and the right people at the right time for all of these changes to have taken place. LaBranche noted that "it hasn't been easy—the Great Recession didn't help," even though it created unexpected opportunities for change. And as Morton pointed out: "We had board leadership that brought a complementary collection of experiences. And they were disciplined and humble enough to never make it about themselves."

4 | Implementing Change

You don't have to see the whole staircase, just take the first step.
—Martin Luther King, Jr., pastor, activist, and humanitarian

When she started her journey as executive director of the National Council of University Research Administrators (NCURA), Kathleen M. Larmett observed:

> We didn't even have what you would call a board of directors. They called themselves an executive committee. It was a good but a slow-moving group. We didn't accomplish a lot: We held an annual meeting, put out a newsletter, conducted a traveling workshop.

> Our board was constituency based—with more than half made up of the chairs of our regional components—rather than based on expertise and skills. The winter meeting consisted of planning the spring meeting. The spring meeting reported on the winter meeting. There was no focus, no strategic planning. They were very insular, there to maintain the status quo.

I was not brought in as a change agent explicitly. I had been there already as staff in the association. But when I interviewed, I did say, "NCURA needs to be more outward focused." The board must have agreed, since they hired me.

Different people react to change in different ways and with different timing. The leaders who introduce and implement change must look at the journey knowing that there will be a significant investment of energy and people-management, and sometimes little understanding at the outset of the timetable or the details of the journey. Change involves implementing a *change process* with clear statements of goals, action steps, and communication. This chapter discusses the change management process, from its initial steps to the process of leading an organization to a new "normal."

Concepts and Application

How to Introduce Organizational Change

Kurt Lewin, often referred to as the father of modern social psychology, states, "If you want to truly understand something, try to change it." This statement is especially true when making changes within or related to an organization or its culture. Change does not only affect policies and procedures within an organization; it radically influences human perceptions of fit and ability to adapt to a new way of doing things (see also Chapter 2). Organizational leaders must determine the type of change necessary in order to adapt to the needs of its internal or external environment.

When thinking about nonprofit governance change, the goal of the first conversation may be to ensure the majority of stakeholders agree that planned change is desired, even if the objectives are not yet clear. A perception must be created that change will lead to better outcomes or results. That conversation might include:

- Identifying the *problems* the organization presently faces. These are the reasons for initiating change. Note that problems are best expressed as real threats the organization is facing, rather than a lack of a specific solution. Solutions come later. For example, as we reported in Chapter 1, some boards and CEOs in our study reported member dissatisfaction, apathetic board members, missed opportunities, and other real threats to their association's future.
- Developing a clear *change vision.* John Bryson (2011), an expert on nonprofit strategic planning, emphasizes the importance of clarifying an organization's mission and vision early in the planning process. Without a clear understanding of the goal, the ensuing planning process may not be productive. This lesson applies equally to change at the board level.
- Carefully articulating and considering the *impact* change will have on the organization, employees, members, and other stakeholders, and planning for it.
- Making a commitment to effectively manage the process through a thoughtful *strategy* for effective change implementation and sustained employee and board commitment. This is also the stage where board members make a commitment to see through the change vision regardless of organizational circumstances. When Pam O'Toole Trusdale of the National Association of Trailer Manufacturers looked back at her organization's journey, she recalled the importance of the moment when one board member said to the others: "We can't let money get in the way of vision."

Starting the Journey of Change

One starts from the status quo. The status quo provides organizations and the people within the organizations a feeling of comfort, familiarity, and safety. Everything's under control. People are often working hard. When there is recognition of needed change, we find that people are often working hard on the wrong things and organizations may be focused on the unclear, unfocused, or unproductive goals or direction. To start the conversation about change, leadership should understand that this will be a deliberate upsetting of the status quo and begin by identifying the reasons for initiating a change and establishing a change vision.

A useful exercise to use to plan the beginning of the change process would be to develop a blueprint of the tasks and action steps (Table 4.1).

Imagining the Future: Visioning Exercise

Have your board members write down the one or two words that describe them *now*, and the one or two words that describe what they would like the board to become in the *future*. When we ran this visioning exercise with focus group attendees—asking them to think retrospectively about their boards before and after the governance changes they led—the results were as shown in Table 4.2. While not everyone so clearly articulated what you see in the table, when we took the objectives provided by some and tried to match them to current situations described by others, the words magically match up as related problems and goal-oriented solutions.

Designing a Change Plan

The next steps are to establish the change plan. Its components can include the following:

1. Establishing a change leadership team
2. Documenting the case for change
3. Developing a preliminary vision for the change
4. Defining the impacts on those affected by the change
5. Creating a preliminary implementation strategy and action plan
6. Identifying measures of success
7. Developing a communication strategy
8. Developing a training strategy
9. Developing an evaluation methodology

Table 4.1   Tasks and Action Steps

Problem	Task	Sample Action Steps
Determine need for change.	What is the problem? (*Examples:* Decision making is slow, factions have formed, board does not speak with one voice.)	Benchmarking research, environmental scan (e.g., SWOT analysis), board self-assessment, process assessments of board meetings.
Establish a change vision.	What is the result we want?	A smaller board size allows more nimbleness, which leads to more effectiveness. By ascertaining what skills, experience, and knowledge are needed on the governing board, the organization strategically builds its board to best serve mission-fulfillment and member needs. See the Visioning Exercise in the next section.
Acknowledge past successes.	What have we done well?	Ask the question: *Historically our board has been successful in the following ways:* _____. This change is designed to build on those successes by recognizing the need for current relevancy and an opportunity to embrace established best practices.
Sound the wake-up call.	If we don't change, what might happen that will create additional problems?	Have an "all-hands-on-deck" meeting. Conduct an environmental scan. Assign tasks. Set deadlines.

(*continued*)

Table 4.1   (*continued*)

Problem	Task	Sample Action Steps
Sell the need for change.	What is our case for change and how can we ensure our stakeholders get it?	Lay out in detail why the change is needed. Focus on the problem, not on potential solutions at this time. Provide data and evidentiary support. Create a sense of urgency.
Appeal to the WIIFM factor.	What are the opportunities for stakeholder groups if we adopt this change?	Define the benefits to change. Personalize as much as possible. Be honest about the changes. For example: *"We will need extra time to change the bylaws but by revising board member selection criteria the board will benefit with a better skillset."*
Watch for and manage the "light bulbs."	How will we know when the light bulb goes on?	Actively monitor reactions. Ascertain *change responses* (see the "Five Cs" framework, discussed later). Create a strategy for engaging those whose light bulbs have not come on yet in additional discussion.

Table 4.2   Good Governance Visioning Exercise

My board is now . . .	I want my board to be . . .
Figurehead	Transformative
Micromanaging	Mission driven
Internally focused	Externally focused
Tactical	Strategic
Fearful	Fearless
Dysfunctional	Competent
Disengaged	Visionary
Entitled	Thoughtful
Risk averse	Risk takers
Frustrated	Effective
Insular	Forward focused
Parochial	Nimble
Operational	Supported
Overwhelmed	Rejuvenated
Ceremonial	Hopeful
Narrow	Flexible
Distrustful	Confident
Confused	Focused
Siloed	Collaborative
Traditional	Evolving
Wimpy	Knowledgeable
Stuck	Learning
Staid	Collegial
Boring	Energized
Unfocused	Targeted

Dealing with Obstacles

We asked our interviewees, "What was most challenging about your governance change?" Respondents could mention as many items as they wished. Our respondents identified seven potential challenges to watch out for in advance of implementing change. Table 4.3 displays

Table 4.3   Challenges Encountered during the Governance Change Process

"What was most challenging about your governance change?"	Number of Respondents Who Mentioned This Problem (of 51 interviews)	Number of Times Challenge Was Mentioned (of 111 items)	Suggested Organizational Responses
Managing emotions	31	50	Communicate clearly and often; practice transparency; identify the old guard and address their concerns (see ahead); build trust in the process; be honest; be patient; let go of ego.
Time, labor, and resources	23	27	Outsource elements of the change process; slow the process down to balance time demands on board and staff; use cash reserves to support change timetable; expand board's capacity to recruit new members so recruitment does not rest on CEO.

Table 4.3 (*continued*)

"What was most challenging about your governance change?"	Number of Respondents Who Mentioned This Problem (of 51 interviews)	Number of Times Challenge Was Mentioned (of 111 items)	Suggested Organizational Responses
Changes to organizational culture	17	20	Create events and opportunities to cement and celebrate the board's new culture; keep tweaking the change process to fit organization's culture; build board–staff and board–board relationships.
Board and staff turnover during change process	7	8	Actively manage board nomination process to identify and retain change champions; invest in board education to bring incoming members up to speed; plan an exit strategy for outgoing board members.
Managing a diversity of perspectives	4	4	Plan new activities to engage membership; communicate actively.
Lack of models and best practices to work from	4	4	Invest in research; attend governance workshops.
No problems reported	2	2	Celebrate and share the story!

the results, the frequency with which the challenge was noted by any single association, and the total number of times the item was mentioned overall.

We also include possible organizational responses to these challenges, most of them offered by the leaders we interviewed. The remainder of this chapter then covers strategies for working through these obstacles. By proactively anticipating these possibilities, change leaders may be able to develop reasonable solutions to manage both organizational culture and personal preferences.

The results reflect a clear pattern of three major challenges and three minor ones, with the most common obstacles being the need to manage change recipients' and agents' emotional reactions to change (expressed by the majority of interviewees). Much of this chapter therefore addresses change management strategies directed at organizational stakeholders. About half of our interviewees also observed that the change involved a great deal of time and labor. They also described how new or old cultures were difficult to manage through the change process (also addressed in this chapter). It's important to emphasize that few interview subjects actually complained about these various challenges—most accepted them as part of the change process—but many remarked that managing the process and emotions tied up in the governance change required more effort than they anticipated. For example:

> One needs to recognize that change takes time and patience. I had to get my ego out of it. I could not be defensive. It wasn't going to be solved with one step. Bringing voices to bear of those who were credible and respected in my organization was critical to effecting change.

Additionally, we heard regional and national associations in particular reporting the challenge of coming to agreement on a governance structure when members represented large geographic areas and a diversity of perspectives. Even within single states, some association leaders described how rural/urban, mountain/coastal, and other geographic distinctions had split their constituencies into factions whose voices were hard to reconcile at the board level. Many of these associations had to shed the historical baggage of constituency-based boards on their way to a stronger governance structure.

We also heard from associations that struggled with forecasting the future when they lacked data or could not find the governance and change management resources they wanted, especially resources accessible online, detailed models for good board meetings, and resources for local and regional associations (since the available resources emphasize national governance needs). We have addressed some of those needs in the following, and also via our suggested references.

In addition to the top-three challenges of emotions, capacity, and culture changes, a minority of respondents experienced the following additional challenges.

Using Knowledge Management to Manage Board Turnover

Some associations found board and staff turnover challenged the change process. They told us that board turnover had two kinds of outcomes. At times it meant that they lost champions prematurely due to term limits, slowing the change process. Lynne Thomas Gordon of AHIMA observed, "It's change management over and over. Some people have already crossed the river and they're looking back wondering why the new people won't even dip their toes in the water." AHIMA's solution was to invest in new-board-member education. At other times term limits required change leaders to wait for resistant board members to term out, also slowing the change process.

Whether due to term limits or through other attrition, the loss of continuity that comes with board turnover can cause stops and starts to any change process. To mitigate this problem, experts recommend the deliberate introduction of *knowledge management* methods. Knowledge management—the management of an organization's intellectual assets—can improve a range of organizational performance characteristics and enable an association to act more intelligently (Gupta et al. 2000). Effective knowledge management enables the communication of knowledge from one person to another so that it can be used in the future regardless of who is at the table (Smith 2001).

Smith (2001) describes two forms of knowledge worth managing during an organizational change: tacit knowledge and explicit knowledge. *Tacit* knowledge is built from experience and resides in our minds. This type of knowledge is often personal and difficult to capture, and it may be dismissed as mere intuition, but it may also yield the most value for organizational growth (Smith 2001, p. 318). *Explicit* knowledge consists of the expertise and experience stored in books, documents, or other physical or electronic formats. This type of knowledge is easy to capture, articulate, and communicate. This book and many other books on association governance represent explicit knowledge, but the knowledge we have documented here comprises a great deal of tacit knowledge that board members and association CEOs shared with us through their stories. The question is: Have they captured and recorded this knowledge for the benefit of future organizational leaders?

Organizations that take the time and energy to develop knowledge management systems can weather board turnover more successfully. A specific example of tacit knowledge management includes taking time to turn tacit knowledge into explicit knowledge by capturing the observations of outgoing board members about effective governance for the benefit of incoming board members (e.g., exit interviews). Smith's (2001) general observations are highly relevant to the board context, since she notes that most work-related explicit knowledge originated as tacit knowledge. Boards use both kinds of knowledge but may have to work harder to capture and codify the tacit knowledge that board members gain through board friendships, mentoring relationships, casual conversations, and other informal exchanges.

Managing Expectations

The big takeaway from this analysis of challenges is that association boards must be prepared to face a sequence of challenges as they manage a change process. Andrew Davidson of the Oregon Association of Hospitals and Health Systems offered this response:

> [What was most challenging?] Expectation management. Not knowing how people were going to react. Managing my own expectations, those of my leadership, those of the rank-and-file membership. . . . It was also difficult in that when you make these changes you tend to get the A Team who wants to serve on the first board. But you have to stagger terms and slot people in for later, too. It becomes a mathematical challenge. . . . Now I am worried as people term off. I have to preserve this great culture even as people turn over.

Or as Christopher Henney, Ohio AgriBusiness Association, stated in reference to dealing with the old guard:

> We haven't lost any members, but we still have some who say, "That's not the way we used to do things."

Those individuals—board, members, or staff—who have benefited from the current way of operating may be unwilling to accept change or new ideas. They may perceive the new governance plans as a real threat to their status and benefits. In fact, in cases where board turnover is part of the plan (to restructure the board's representation, bring on new skills, etc.) some board members may lose their seats and some members may feel their influence will be diminished. They have a legitimate role in the process, but managing it can be difficult.

Addressing the old guard involves frank "What's In It For Me?" (W.I.I.F.M) discussions. Be honest about what the changes could mean for them but be sure to define the benefits to change and what the likely positive outcomes will be. Personalize the benefits as much as possible. This will take time, patience, and communication. Additionally, be prepared for compromise respecting the pace of change. Many of the cases we studied involved associations that slowed down governance changes to allow their board membership to turn over, or to allow old-guard board members a graceful exit via the careful structuring and implementation of term limits. Organizations that recognize these tradeoffs will weather change better and preserve the most desirable elements of their present culture.

Staff can represent the old guard, too, since they have their established management routines. Terry Storm, of the Pikes Peak Association of REALTORS®, told us:

> The staff were the ones who questioned a new governance model more than the board. They thought that it would be more work than before. They actually ended up doing less because they didn't have to staff nearly as many board committees. It made everything a lot more effective.

As this comment demonstrates, documenting and demonstrating that a new strategy has organizational benefits can help staff recognize the value of change. The "Five Cs" change response framework described later in this chapter can be used to help staff adapt to a new culture, most especially to observe how staff can be incentivized and rewarded for coming on board.

Managing a New Board Culture

Change management requires attending to a shifting organizational and board culture (i.e., one that is more consensual, strategic, casual, formal, professional, collegial, consultative, active, etc.). Board members and staff must define the desired aspects, behaviors, and processes of the new culture. Understanding what actually needs to change, raising consciousness, being explicit about expectations, coaching change recipients, not assuming everyone will get it at the same time or, for some, at all, crafting a deliberate process, and incentivizing adaptation all help to create "the tipping point" when a new culture becomes the majority culture. For further reading, the nonprofit consulting firm Bridgespan (2011) offers specific strategies for managing the process on its website.

Maintaining Momentum: Gladwell's "Tipping Points"

After new goals are defined and momentum has been achieved, change leaders must continue to reinforce new ways of doing things to engrain new cultural habits. Chris McEntee, CEO of American Geophysical Union, recalled that point: "We were still in a somewhat fragile place. You can easily fall into old habits of doing things, so we spent a lot of time at that first meeting of the board asking ourselves, 'What does this really mean?'"

Malcolm Gladwell's (2000) widely read observations on "tipping points" include three key factors that he suggests are crucial to success. Similarly to Ross and Segal (2002), Gladwell first notes the contributions early adapters and other change champions make in creating momentum. Our interviewees described how they instituted specific strategies for giving champions a bigger voice in the process, including asking them to speak at board and membership meetings, and to participate in visits to chapters. For example, Peg Smith of the American Camp Association described the effort to recruit new board members:

> We thought, "Who are the other champions across the country who also have positive reputations, who were viewed well in our community, who were passionate about our mission, and who could bring those additional thoughts and values?"

The second element, Gladwell's "stickiness factor," describes the undefinable and sometimes out-of-the-box events, actions, or behaviors that are compelling enough to get others to focus on the something new or different. For example, the American Geophysical Union board included a role-playing exercise in which they took themselves outside of their organization and pretended that they were in the White House. The American Dental Education Association added a "Day of Learning" at board retreats, which were designed in turn to get board members "outside of their dental box" and to engage in thinking differently about leading their profession.

The third factor is context, the recognition that the environment in which change is to take place can offer powerful support. From our consulting careers, we recalled a key board meeting in which a CEO simply suggested moving the meeting. The room that had been used for several years had no outside windows, and seating around the table was tight. The second room had a beautiful view over a body of water, and the table and setup were far more conducive to dialogue and conversation. The result was that the tone of the meeting was immediately different and contributed to the adoption of new strategies for the organization.

Culture is a squishy term, and raising board member consciousness regarding the need to strengthen a board's culture (of accountability, professionalism, transparency, etc.) may be challenging. Nonetheless, we know it's an important task if only because the "high-performing" organizational literature we listed in our Introduction mentions "culture" so frequently. Jim Collins wrote more about culture than anything else in his analysis of high-performing businesses in *Good to Great*. ASAE (2006) did the same for membership organizations in *7 Measures of Success* as did Leslie Crutchfield and Heather Grant (2008) in *Forces for Good*. In the governance context, simple policy questions such as "What decisions remain with the board and what belong to staff?" have a cultural dimension that must be addressed in the course of arriving at an answer (Gazley 2015).

Managing Data (or Lack Thereof)

Change also needs a good evidence base. Some change recipients may advocate for the status quo (or even for an unwise change) based on a certain perception or even spin of data. In other cases, they may rely solely on opinion rather than data. Strategic change leaders should anticipate both events and think through the role that data (or lack thereof) may play in dialogue and decision-making processes to avoid possible snags.

In our interviews, we found associations that weathered change successfully also brought (or quickly developed) a culture of performance measurement at both organizational and board levels. A key to using data effectively in change management is to ensure that the methodology to create the data is sound, the data are presented as clearly and succinctly as possible, and the discussion about implications and courses of action is objective and unemotional.

Managing the Illusion of Democracy

A point that emerged in just a few interviews and one focus group is that boards create power dynamics (over staff, members, and themselves) by virtue of their legal authority in an organization. We found association leaders wrestling with what these power dynamics meant during governance changes. In a provocative essay in *Nonprofit Quarterly*, Chao Guo (2012) has observed that "relatively little attention has been paid to . . . the embedded power dynamics that influence . . . whose voices get heard and whose get left out." Guo's point is not that a "democratic deficit" exists in all boards but rather that many boards are not actively discussing or creating processes to decide how to govern democratically.

As boards restructure, a window of opportunity appears to open for such a conversation. Some change leaders found, for example, that their original "representative" model of governance had not been achieving its desired objective of engaging members. At the Society of Teachers of Family Medicine (STFM), Executive Director Stacy Brungardt, CAE, recalled that as STFM restructured its governance, "we wanted to embrace the idea of member input but weren't set up for it." Other association leaders recalled the challenges of incorporating an honest discussion about "shared governance"—a hallmark of member-serving associations—into the governance planning. Even when decisions to assign stronger fiduciary authority to the governing board resulted in less direct member power, they reported success in retaining *meaningful* membership representation in governance, but only after investing heavily in hearing member perspectives about the changes.

Anticipating Reactions to Governance Change Using the "Five Cs" Framework

Connie Wootton of the Southwestern Association of Episcopal Schools (see full case later in this chapter) notes that as they began to work on governance, the board's biggest challenge was diversity of thought from members representing a large multi-state region. Even individuals from a homogeneous group can react to change differently. Bernard Ross and Clare Segal (2002) have described five possible reactions to change. These five characterizations of change recipients and their influence on organizational dynamics have emerged from their careers in organizational development consulting (for more go to www.managementcentre.co.uk/).

Many of our case studies describe individuals who could be characterized under this framework (i.e., a champion of change, convert, challenger, and so on). Readers may not find that recipients of change in their organization neatly fall into a typology of five, but this framework is useful in helping change leaders anticipate possible responses to change. We have adapted Ross's and Segal's suggestions for engaging each kind of change recipient to the context of governance change, adding strategies we found our interviewees using. The principal conclusion we make is that being proactive about identifying and predetermining how to possibly engage each type of individual will help to move the process along and avoid potential derailment:

1. **Champions** describe those who most easily embrace new ideas and accept the risks of change (see also Gladwell 2000). While they are crucial to success, Ross and Segal (2002) suggest that champions should be employed carefully as change agents, since some may lack objectivity and may be greeted with skepticism by others. They may not always offer organizational leadership the constructive feedback it needs or thoroughly challenge the merits of new strategies. Involving them in governance workshops may help those individuals acquire a more realistic view about the pace of the governance change process. Nevertheless, champions should be, and will expect to be, involved. To engage champions constructively, our interview subjects ensured they also learned about best practices, and sent them to research governance models, sit on bylaws revision committees, speak to others, or secure necessary external resources.

2. **Chasers** will be slower to join up than champions, but Ross and Segal suggest they may offer organizational leadership a more accurate idea of how acceptable a new proposal will be. They should be given an opportunity to discuss new ideas with others before forming a judgment. They may look to key opinion makers in the organization for guidance. But once they do, they should be engaged in the change process because they will move the organization toward the tipping point when the majority of individuals accept the change. Our interview subjects described change processes that gave chasers access to key organizational thought leaders. They emphasized their responsibility to share information with change recipients about what was known or unknown about the anticipated impacts of the change. Open communication with these individuals will pay off in greater ownership and co-creation of the change vision.

3. **Converts** may form the largest group of change recipients, but they may be the hardest to engage and to read. They may not ever speak up. They may also take a long time to embrace new ideas. As boards restructure, converts may be found among board members, staff members, and the association's membership ranks. In a few cases, association leaders recounted change processes that were uneventful. But not everyone can be expected to come on board immediately.

Strategies for engaging converts include offering them opportunities to listen and to ask questions of organizational leadership.
The concerns of converts—including the "what's in it for me?"
details—should be anticipated, if possible, and addressed in these
communications. Leaders should provide opportunities for both
individual and group active listening. No one should be talked out
of their feelings.

We saw these principles reflected in the heavy investment the
association's leaders whom we interviewed had made in communicating with all stakeholder groups. Organizational leaders also
practiced active outreach about both the change process and its
goals to effectively reach this group. We also saw leaders slowing
down the pace of change to accommodate converts. According to
Ross and Segal, the advantage of taking more time and effort with
converts is that as slow as they are to adopt new ideas, they may
embrace them more permanently. Thus, timing the change
process at a pace acceptable to the converts can give a change
process much greater momentum in the long run.

4. **Challengers** may comprise a smaller group but may demand the
greatest effort. They may include individuals who will recognize
the benefits of the change eventually but have been poorly
socialized about how to confront change effectively. Board members may be executives in their professions and not have had much
experience with consensus decision making. In AOTA's case, as
referenced earlier, they described some of their board members
finally getting "religion." We also heard from Dennis Simmons,
then-CEO of Southwestern Automated Clearing House
Association:

> An obstacle was people's vision about how the process
> should unfold—individual opinion versus consensus deci-
> sion making. Most of the members are senior executives of
> their own organizations, so they are used to getting their
> own way.

Experts advise "holding up a mirror" to help these individuals
take a step back and understand the effects of their behavior on
the board's work. As our interviews revealed, disruptions to the

process can be expected, and dealing with challengers can involve periods of stagnation and reversals. When challenges are raised, the first step in finding a successful resolution is recognizing that a person's actions or behaviors usually stem from something specific, whether it is ignorance, misunderstanding, a personality conflict, or a deeper issue. This response is predicated on the assumption that a second step will occur—that leadership will intervene directly, humanely, with unity, and in a timely way. If leadership doesn't guide the process, the trouble could be left unattended and may result in a worse outcome (Kissman 2006).

Our interview subjects described efforts (not always successful) to actively engage challengers on both emotional and cognitive levels to identify the stakes they felt they had in the outcome and understand how to address their expectations. As Ross and Segal have observed, some of our interview subjects reported that challengers caused them to more thoroughly think through possible obstacles and articulate the benefits of a change. But organizations should also anticipate and preempt the most negative aspects of the challenger personality by creating formal rules about the change process in advance to ensure the process is not derailed by objections.

5. **Changephobes** are defined by Ross and Segal as a small group who may never be convinced of the benefits of a new idea. They can be immovable. And if these individuals actively oppose the change, they may lower morale, as some of our stories recounted. The association leaders we studied described a range of disruptive reactions from changephobes, including some who publicly accused the change agents of power grabs, some who ran for a board seat expressly to stop a change process or who initiated parliamentary or procedural challenges, and some who attempted "back-door" maneuvers in attempts to weaken the change leaders.

How these individuals are addressed during a governance change may depend on their number, the strength of their resistance, and the credibility of their perspective. Ross and Segal suggest they be removed as quickly as possible, but this advice does not fit the context of governance. For example, we frequently found that the strongest opposition to board change came from former board members. Therefore, we recommend caution. Changephobes are still stakeholders and should still be treated respectfully, and offered honest information about the planned change. Board members who oppose change should be offered the opportunity to complete their terms. As Kissman (2006) has observed,

> No one enjoys confrontation, especially with regard to a professional colleague. Successfully working in a group context is highly dynamic and can engender great passion and emotion when disagreements or conflicts erupt. Paying attention to these dynamics and actively honoring the human element requires commitment and work.

Recognizing resistance, trying to see the situation through the other lens, and then actively addressing resistance head-on is often the only way to defuse it. Communicate, educate about the value of the proposed changes, find ways to allow obstructionists feedback about their concerns, and find points of natural agreement to create a foundation on which to build. Gentle persistence and active management with individuals who are resistant is key. Even then, taking the pressure off increases the likelihood of falling into old patterns of behavior.

Assuming the strategies suggested for dealing with challengers have been attempted, we suggest three means of addressing insurmountable opposition, based on our interviews with governance change leaders: (1) Employ association bylaws to remove the resisting individuals, (2) employ term limits to create board turnover, and (3) sideline and ignore the opposition if you have a clear mandate to move forward. In this last case, it is sometimes sufficient to simply let the challenger know that he or she is outvoted and that sustained resistance will not be valuable to the organization. Leadership can say directly, "We respect your right to your opinion. But because you feel this way and the group feels another, perhaps this is not the board you should be serving on." Giving challengers a graceful way out serves all.

Summary

Understanding the concepts of change, from the need to formally introduce it with deliberateness and communication, to the value of creating a change plan, to managing the journey, and to having an awareness that different individuals will react in different ways is critical to the journey of transformational change and high-performing governance. Woody Wiedenhoeft, executive director of the Wisconsin Association of School Business Officials, perfectly described this deliberative journey of planning, evaluation, and more planning:

> It has been a story of steps. Each step has added to our journey as far as becoming more productive and accountable to the membership. It has actually been hard work by our volunteer board members. Each year we get a little better at it. In a nutshell, a lot has been created because our board has been sensitive in having strategic discussions and multiyear planning, follow-up, and evaluation.

Doing the necessary homework and groundwork before starting down the path is critical where deliberate change is planned; dedicating thought and process in whatever way is possible in the case of unplanned change will also help achieve success. Even when an organization finds itself needing to react to the unplanned event, taking as much time as may be possible to be more thoughtful and proactive in a response will ultimately bring about a preferred result.

While board members and CEOs cannot be expected to be psychologists or therapists, they do need to understand that managing change for success will take active people management and team building. The single biggest challenge in any transformation may simply be getting people to change their behaviors. To succeed in any transformational effort, leaders must get people to see and feel the benefits of change.

Both cases that follow reflect these lessons. In the first, the National Council of University Research Administrators board members had to convince other members that unwelcome governance changes were in the association's best interests. In the second, the Southwestern Association of Episcopal Schools worked through some difficult times by building a board that was accepting of change.

Collegiality Converts Challengers

Case: National Council of University Research Administrators

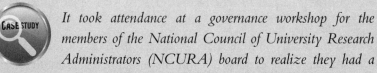

It took attendance at a governance workshop for the members of the National Council of University Research Administrators (NCURA) board to realize they had a problem. Fifteen years later, at another workshop, they were held up as an exemplar of good governance. In between was a carefully planned process and hard work at bylaws revision as NCURA realized the period of expansion and innovation the organization was enjoying would not continue without a stronger board.

NCURA was established in 1959 to "advance the field of research administration through education and professional development programs, the sharing of knowledge and experience, and by fostering a professional, collegial, and respected community" (www.ncura.edu/AboutUs.aspx).

Reflecting NCURA's collegial culture, five individuals joined our interview to reflect on the association's journey to good governance: Kathleen M. Larmett, executive director; Vivian Holmes, board president; Pat Hawk, immediate past president; Kim Moreland, past president and a board member during the governance transition described ahead; and Christina Hansen, also a board member during the transition.

Larmett was promoted from a staff position to executive director at the end of 1997. Moreland recalled:

We didn't hire Kathleen as a change agent, but it was the end of a phase of growth for the board and we knew she was needed. Having an executive director to lead a group of volunteers through this was essential. We in leadership were willing to make change but didn't know how to do it.

Challenge: NCURA Discovers It Has a Problem

Larmett's first strategy was to learn:

The first thing I did was join ASAE and find a workshop for CEOs. I took my board president, Mary Husemoller, with me. After about the first hour in this workshop our eyes were opened. It was huge for my president to sit in a room with leaders from 40 other associations and hear their stories; I had seen other associations but she had not. Our facilitator, Bud Crouch of Tecker International, LLC, said, "If you took all your board minutes from the past five years and asked your members to take a high lighter and mark up what they thought was important, how much highlight would you see?" We looked at each other and said, "We have a problem!" We hired Bud and flew the entire board in for a one-day boot camp at the Dulles Marriott. We all became a band of brothers and sisters that day.

> *Our facilitator said "If you took all your board minutes from the past five years and asked your board members to take a highlighter and mark up what they thought was important, how much highlight would you see?" We looked at each other and said "We have a problem!"*

(*continued*)

(continued)

Strategy: Start the Process

Continues Larmett:

We decided we needed to make membership and financial improvements. We held another two-day meeting in Philadelphia with Bud. The first day was visioning; the second day was strategic planning. We had done strategic planning before. But this launched a much bigger effort.

The following winter board meeting we sat down and started to do the really hard work of taking apart the governance structure to redo it, modernize it. We decided we wanted open, competitive elections. We shrank the board, creating four at-large members and eight geographic members, five nationally elected officers, and the immediate past president. And we added a unique twist: The president could also appoint up to three additional voting board members based on strategic needs.

According to Christina Hansen:

What was really clear to me before the governance change is that we had grown but we were not able to be flexible to recognize the kinds of changes we were seeing in our membership, such as a growing number of departmental administrators and women in the profession. We were growing, but we had no targets. The board was mired in the day-to-day activities of the association but hadn't created a vision for the organization. We were growing but we had no targets. The board hadn't created a vision for the organization.

Challenge: Maintaining Momentum

We got stalled a couple of times, so had to go back and revisit the strategic plan and our wish list. We re-crafted our bylaws, slimming them way down for flexibility. But we eventually pulled through. We passed the bylaws in November 1999 and held our first new board meeting in 2000.

Strategy: Get Buy-In from Membership

The change in the first five years was dramatic. Our president went out to every regional meeting that spring and got buy-in from a majority of our membership. Our board is really well oiled now. They understand collegiality, respect, fiduciary duties. The investment has been well worth it.

NCURA's board members concurred. Moreland noted:

One of the wisest things we did was take this plan out to the regions and membership. They had little idea of what we were sitting on. This was a chance for

We needed flexibility. Previously ideas would get stuck in standing committees and not arrive at the full board until it was too late.

us to educate them on the inner workings of the board. In those early days, as Kathleen says, we were using the staff as administrative assistants and using the board as an executive director. Once the membership understood where we were going, it built a groundswell of support that allowed us to move forward with confidence.

Strategy: Create a Flexible Governance Model

Larmett, the CEO, recalled:

I remember one two-and-a-half-day meeting in New Orleans that got us into some difficult conversations as we tore apart and

(continued)

(*continued*)

> streamlined the bylaws. We [discovered we] needed flexibility. Previously ideas would get stuck in standing committees and not arrive at the full board until it was too late.

Challenge: Angry Past Presidents

> But there was resistance. The most challenging was the fear of change. You do hear people say "it ain't broke." It was a constant PR push forward. We had some angry past presidents. [For them] it was painful to see any tinkering at all. They started e-mail campaigns to oppose the change. They took it personally, like it was a referendum on them.

Larmett notes that this opposition originated over disagreements about the need for change:

> They perceived that it was a thriving organization and felt it was risky to change something thriving. We all believed the organization was a good one. We just thought it could be *great*.

Strategy: Recruit Champions to Convert the Challengers

> So we had to get some other board leaders to write articles in the newsletter to promote the changes and address the objections. I remembered thinking to myself, "Don't be afraid to lose your job." I was nervous before that big vote. There is nothing like a group of angry past presidents. We had other board members (peer to peer) take the objectors out into the hall and try to talk through their concerns. But when the vote passed it was very affirming.

The regional compo-
nents also had to create or
change their own bylaws to
effect this change. Some of

> *There is nothing like a group of angry past presidents.*

the regions didn't even have bylaws. Because the new rules stated they had to be compliant with our bylaws, we had to teach them how to write bylaws.

Strategy: Keep Process Consistent with Organization's Culture

NCURA has a mission and culture that respects academic freedom, so the association had to accept the pushback it received from members as a normal response. While the board felt it needed to honor full and inclusive membership engagement in decision making, change was able to happen because of the growing recognition that NCURA's board had fiduciary duties of loyalty and obedience they needed to abide by.

Former President Pat Hawk observed: "I am not sure anyone had previously connected the dots on this."

Christina Hansen:

I was one of the more resistant board members. I remember sitting in the room and really disagreeing with some of the sugges-tions. But I saw the light. The fact that we were so

> *I remember sitting in the room and really disagreeing with some of the suggestions. But I saw the light. The best conversations we had were putting big audacious goals on the table.*

visionary helped me. The best conversations we had were putting big audacious goals on the table.

(continued)

(*continued*)

CEO Larmett picked up the narrative:

When the vote went out to the membership, it was almost unanimously in favor. But some people said, "That's not how we do it at our university." And we had to explain board decisions are different.

Ninety-five percent of the pushback has now gone away. There are now so many more benefits than there were fifteen years ago. People realized that the changes were done for the benefit of everyone in the organization and the profession.

Strategy: Clarify National and Regional Roles

Christina Hansen described how the change also required NCURA to clarify national and regional roles:

Another thing we intended to do through the restructuring was expand the involvement of members. That point was initiated during the governance discussion in the regions. It was important to be clear about the national board's responsibilities as well as how the regions would be involved. So the regions ended up as stronger partners in the new plan.

Larmett noted how the change democratized membership involvement: "That was also the year when we did our first open call for volunteers. It was previously very political. We had a reputation as an old boys' club. After that call, everyone felt they had more opportunity to participate."

Kim Moreland agreed: "Yes, it became 'our' organization. I remember the before and after. Before, it felt provincial, like a smoke-filled room. To see the difference today is pretty powerful."

Larmett described the results as very positive:

In the first 10 years our membership grew from 3,000 to 7,000. We went from five programs a year before including our annual meeting to over 50 programs after. We went from a four-page to a 25-page newsletter to a 75-page full-color magazine. We started electronic programming that our members could download.

Strategy: Board Development

Larmett continued:

Our board was great, all good people. But we needed to teach ourselves board work. Today, every year there's a formal orientation of board members. We also talk about the history and culture of the organization, board behavior. And we also decided to invest in an Executive Leadership Program. It's a finishing school or master's-level program in executive leadership for our members. It's really important right now not to become complacent. So our Executive Leadership Program is for our association's future leaders. They go to training for emotional intelligence, working with others, governance, and so on. It is very expensive, a big investment for us. But when I polled our board recently we discovered over half of the board members had been through this program.

Vivian Holmes noted how important training in board leadership has become to NCURA's future:

In our Executive Leadership Program we go over the "this is what the board does." A lot of us in university settings don't necessarily know what that looks like. So there's now stability in our structure for people.

(continued)

(continued)
Challenge: Maintaining Momentum When Things Are Going Well

The group discussed the strategies most critical to their success, most particularly the need to maintain progress when things go well. Larmett observed:

> When things go poorly, you can rally the troops. When things are successful, it can be harder to motivate people to strive for more. We accomplished this through board orientation and training, to ensure they know their responsibilities. At this past board meeting I had them put out a timeline to look at what we've done, and they were awestruck. That gave us confidence to start a new plan.

In the end, Kim Moreland credits determination with the positive outcome: "This all had a lot to do with a determination to improve ourselves. To take an old organization and figure out how to do it better."

Accepting Change at the Right Pace Pays Off

Case: Southwestern Association of Episcopal Schools

 This is a story of incremental change built on a realization that the comfort of the status quo was no longer serving the mission of the organization. The board changes at Southwestern Association of Episcopal Schools involved no catalyzing events but rather an organic bow to changing constituent needs. But when an unexpected national event polarized the membership and challenged the board to respond, the leaders of the organization found that their evolution to a representative board with a strong culture of respect served them well.

The mission of the Southwestern Association of Episcopal Schools (SAES) is "to lead, nurture, and unify Episcopal schools in order to advance educational excellence within the faith community of the Episcopal Church." SAES serves 118 schools that are richly diverse in location, size, and scope. On its website, SAES takes pride in the fact that it is recognized by state educational agencies and is the single religious affiliated accrediting association recognized by NAIS and the only Episcopal accrediting association in the United States (www.swaes.org/page.cfm?p=498).

Challenge: Clubby but Comfortable Board

Prior to becoming SAES's executive director, Connie Wootton had served as head of one of its member schools and as a member of its board. As noted by Wootton earlier in this chapter:

(continued)

(*continued*)

Before our governance retooling, the board members of SAES were whoever you could talk into it. It was a little incestuous. If we were really honest about it, we liked it that way. We looked forward to seeing the same people every year. We floated along.

Our big change came about when I asked, "Should we have term limits?" This would have been a sweeping change for us. And everyone feared the change because we were pretty comfortable. Instituting term limits would mean losing some long-standing board members. We spent the better part of three years easing into this. There wasn't any anger; it was more of a concern and a worry that we would hurt some of our board members in this process.

Challenge: Need for Broad Geographic Representation

For SAES, the next big change was to think about broader board issues like greater and more deliberate geographic representation. But Wootton also described the board's biggest challenge as its diversity of thought. SAES represents a large region. Getting members together geographically when the board only met a couple of times a year was a challenge. Wootton recalled,

That change was also a little frightening. But we realized after instituting term limits, we still had 10 fingers and 10 toes, so then we could think about other changes. We were determined to again take it slow to do least harm. I think it was the right speed.

Wootton explained:

It was all about having good discussions. We did bring in consultants with strategic planning expertise intermittently but mostly it's been the generative discussion of the board; they were the ones who put these changes in place. Most of them are leaders in their own right—heads of school or church—so we have benefited from the leadership training they have already had, which included board development training. They have differing viewpoints but that hasn't made it challenging; it's only made the discussion richer. We intended to be a well-developed board. The new representatives have a voice to bring to the table. They have strengthened the voice of the whole association.

Challenge: Hands-Off Board

Dr. Susan Lair, who serves as head of a school in Houston, was in the chair's seat during this process. Lair recalls:

I've been board chair for four years. We didn't have a hands-on or micromanaging board before. It was the opposite. Our former board was too hands-off. We had an excellent executive director in Connie and we just let her do her job. And our board had not seriously taken its job of governing as their responsibility. Connie had to do not only day-to-day management of operations and stewardship of our accreditation process, but also much of the actual leading of the board and its process—developing the agenda for meetings, preparing the action items, coordinating committees—all the heavy lifting. Our board members just came to the meetings. It was a sweet little place, not very well respected, but everyone felt happy.

We had really good conversations when we were implementing these changes and amending our bylaws. When we brought in

(continued)

(*continued*)

consultants to work with us, that helped. We focused on what's the responsibility of the board and what's the responsibility of the executive director in terms of mission fulfillment.

Strategy: Redefine the Board's Role

We determined that for SAES, the board job was to ensure identification of standards and that they are fulfilled in the accreditation process. It was all about focusing on our mission. We help our children learn character. So the board began to work at strengthening our procedures for accreditation. The board today makes sure our member schools know about best practices and how to be an excellent faith-based school. Now we make sure that our member schools are good. We hold schools accountable. Kids only have one shot at third grade and they deserve a great experience.

Lair also credits the culture of the organization, particularly the fact that it is faith-based, as having a lot to do with the success of the process for instituting the changes:

Our organization had a sense of comradery. We had the ability to call another head and talk about issues and problems facing us— genuine conversations, helpful advice. There was no sense of competition in our group.

Today, while the SAES board still only meets officially twice a year, the governing body has tasked numerous committees to meet to carry on the work of oversight. The board also changed how its membership did things. Routine stuff is now dealt with electronically. There is active agenda management to focus on generative and strategic issues. Wootton and Lair talk often but, as Lair reports, appropriately so:

Connie uses me and others on the board as a sounding board or to connect with or help specific schools with governance or operational challenges they are facing. But other than that, we do our job and she does hers.

Challenge: Politics Causes Rift in Membership

In 2003, a national political event challenged the SAES board to lean hard on the better culture the organization's leadership had forged. The first openly gay bishop was consecrated by the Episcopal Church. The decision led multiple Episcopal parishes and individuals to split with the Episcopal Church of America. Wootton explained the challenge for SAES:

When a parish splits, what happens to the school? On what side of the issue do we fall? Do we practice what we preach regarding tolerance? It was a real struggle because we had board members with strong views either way. I wondered if this issue might be where our train would leave the track. But because we already respected each other, we didn't [fall apart] because we listened to each other. We decided there wasn't only one way. Our decision was if a school wanted to stay with us even if the parish left the church, we would continue to accredit the school.

We still lost three schools over this because the schools were in such conservative places that they couldn't continue to remain with Episcopal Church of America. It was rough. We are in the Bible Belt. The fact that we are coming in with an accreditation standard that says "you cannot exclude a student based on sexual orientation" was hard.

(*continued*)

(continued)
Strategy: Mission–Driven Decisions

Lair added:

It caused a huge rift in our faith and we really had to wrestle with that. The schools that were involved needed an organization such as SAES. We had to come to grips with what it means to be a faith-based origination on all its levels. We grew from this as a board because we were able to deal with it from a culture of respect. We came to the decision to deal with it school by school. Because of our conversations and the way we handled ourselves, by not getting personal, it was wonderful.

In another instance, one member school withdrew a student with lesbian parents. We had some board members who said, "Cut (the school) loose right now." But it wasn't so simple; a teacher in our school earns credit for service only when teaching in a state-accredited school. So, if we withdraw accreditation, we cause teachers to lose credit. And students also lose academic credits.

This was an emotionally charged issue to be considered by such a diverse geographic area. We had hardliners, some of the most influential and highly respected on board, who were determined to cut the discriminatory schools loose. We did cut one school, but at the end of the day, we voted to carry the school for up to two years until it could get accredited by somebody else.

The situation made us examine who we are. The bottom line is that we are part of the EC of A, closely aligned with them, and are going to uphold the respect of dignity for every human being regardless of sexual orientation. So it was a strong mission-driven decision all along; it just took a long time. It was unanimous in the end.

Strategy: Succession Planning

A big change coming up is Wootton's pending retirement as CEO in 2015. But the board, with its newfound leadership skills, is supervising a professional and well-managed search process.

Lair observed:

> Connie and I talked about her retirement two years ago, so we developed a plan to give SAES plenty of time to prepare for the transition and conduct a search. She will be hard to replace. She knows governance and she knows operations.

Wootton concluded: "My big takeaway from our experience was to try not to rush things. Let board members adjust."

5 | Leading Sideways
Influencing Change within the Board

The key to successful leadership is influence, not authority.
— Kenneth H. Blanchard

Carol Finn, former president of the board of directors of the American Geophysical Union, heard the question loud and clear: *Why would we even think about doing anything?* She recalls:

> When I became secretary/treasurer in 2008, we had a solid foundation: a good balance sheet, publications, staff, and a world-class meeting. But we weren't prepared for the future. I heard, "Why would you even think about doing anything?" But the flipside to all the "good" was the fact that there was no direction. We were living in the past. We were the world's largest association of earth and space scientists, with over 60,000 members in 140 countries, and we were stuck.

"Stuck" was characterized by a governing board unaware of its responsibilities and therefore not strategic, with little fiduciary oversight and no foresight. The strategic plan sat on a shelf. Overall, the organization was unresponsive to member issues. Because decisions were made and information was held by one or two people (out of a staff of 200), volunteers were often uninformed about how AGU worked. There were an unusual number of staff complaints. Staff and volunteers did not have the right tools for the job; the organization had outgrown the internal systems it was using. There was no succession plan or knowledge management.

As you will see demonstrated by AGU's case at the end of this chapter, when boards lead their own transformational change, they face at least two challenges: They must be able to make successful *collective* decisions, and they must be able to disassociate themselves from the more emotional aspects of the change, particularly in those instances when their personal preference is not part of a decision. Neither of these skills may come naturally to board members. To support the process, this chapter introduces theories of team dynamics and briefly describes the two best opportunities board members have to educate themselves about their responsibilities: through the orientation of new board members and through ongoing board development.

Ideally, a board has invested in team-building and governance education well ahead of any challenging, wholesale change. Our interviews suggest strongly that these boards had more successful change processes. However, when compared to team-building, it is formal board development and training that is likely to be the more familiar aspect of "good governance" to board members. The general nonprofit evidence suggests that team building and other efforts to build a culture of shared governance are lagging.

For example, Gazley and Bowers (2013) found 62 percent of membership associations had a formal orientation for new board members, but only 17 percent had a mentoring system to match new and experienced board members. And 30–40 percent of association boards invested in training, professional development of the CEO in good governance, or grooming of future board officers.

BoardSource (2013) found that 71 percent of surveyed members had a structured board member orientation. But half of these nonprofit organizations reported boardroom conversations were dominated by a few individuals, and only half of board members effectively coached one another to develop their strengths.

Concepts and Application

Supporting Board-Led Change through Team Building

A board is not a natural team. It comprises a disparate group of individuals who don't necessarily have much in common and, aside from serving on the board, may never have crossed paths (Kissman 2006). Further, a board's composition and responsibilities may change at stages of the organization's lifecycle. As Chait and colleagues (2005) observe, external events may require boards to frame stronger fiduciary, strategic, or generative ways of governing depending on circumstances. The need for a board to evolve and to work collectively is why a proactive understanding of team theory is helpful (see also the Tools section of this book's appendix).

Team theories can be used to describe many elements of board dynamics. We address here just one theory of teams with close associations to change management. Experts describe team formation as a process of group development that has patterns of productivity and conflict that can be managed if understood (LaFasto and Larson 2001; Whelan 2005). These clear patterns have helped experts on team dynamics produce easily understandable frameworks for helping team managers achieve higher productivity (see, for example, Tuckman and Jensen's 1977 "Forming, Storming, Norming" framework in the Tools section of the appendix).

Successful teams of all kinds also hold their members accountable by using team ground rules and communications guidelines. Rules help team members take ownership of results, prevent misunderstandings, and avoid conflicts. Applying this lesson to governance, boards also develop formal agreements among members about the process of governing (Eadie 2004). While a sample board member agreement is included in the Tools section of the appendix, experts would recommend using this as a starting place only and dedicating additional board time to reflect on what is actually needed of each other in service on a particular board.

The process of team-building within boards is best understood as an ongoing, not intermittent effort. This feature of strong boards was reflected in some of our cases. Borrowing lessons from the champion coach, Phil Jackson (Jackson and Delahanty 2014):

> Basketball is a great mystery. You can do everything right. You can have the perfect mix of talent and the best system of offense in the game. . . . But if the players don't have a sense of oneness as a group, your efforts won't pay off. And the bond that unites a team can be so fragile, so elusive. Oneness is not something you can turn on with a switch. You need to create the right environment for it to grow, then nurture it carefully every day.

Orientation and Education

After a new member is elected, orientation offers a valuable opportunity to acculturate the new member to the board and clarify expectations (Eadie 2004). Kissman (2006) has observed that difficult board member behavior often originates in failures of the recruitment, orientation, onboarding, and ongoing training process. To make the most effective collective decisions, boards should be guided by up-to-date bylaws, a board manual, a regularly reviewed conflict-of-interest policy, and a code of ethics. Most surprising to Kissman (2006, p. xi) in her research was that "most boards and CEOS readily acknowledge that boards had not done this work due to time constraints or fear of insulting already-courted board member candidates."

Board member orientation is one of the easiest and most effective ways not only to ward off potential challenges but to best position an incoming board member to acclimate to a high-performing team. Now an established best practice, many of the organizations interviewed in this study reported implementing formal board orientation opportunities as part of their journey to high performance. (BoardSource's Board Orientation chart is included in the Tools section of the appendix.)

Board training can include not only the initial formal orientation but also job descriptions, hiring of consultants and trainers, mentoring, retreats, and other forms of board development. Board development can also include training for chief staff in supporting board members effectively (Gazley and Bowers 2013). The case of the National Association of Trailer Manufacturers (NATM) emphasizes the possible payoff. Beginning with a planning retreat, NATM's board invested heavily in training and learning. As Pam O'Toole Trusdale, NATM executive director, observed, this relatively young organization realized that to professionalize its membership the board had to professionalize itself. They achieved this goal through active membership in BoardSource, webinars, and workshops, including adapting elements of the Policy Governance® model. Trusdale described the result as "dramatic" as the board "turned from reactive to proactive" in its duties.

> *To professionalize its membership the board had to professionalize itself.*

Summary

The lessons we heard from our interviews reinforce the point that team building, orientation, and education of board members create strong board cultures that facilitate governance change and prevent problems. All of the cases in this book, not only those following this chapter, describe board education activities. But only some describe board-building efforts. As the cases of Delta Sigma Phi and the

American Geophysical Union illustrate, establishing a common vision for excellence pulled the board together to want to "be the best" and this started with understanding and implementing governance best practices. The Tools section of the appendix of this book includes a number of helpful resources for board members to increase governance effectiveness such as active team-building to set expectations of one another.

Leveraging Intention to Create Governance Change

Case: Delta Sigma Phi

 Today, Delta Sigma Phi has "velocity." But it didn't always. Learn how a traditional men's fraternity acquired a more successful meaning of governance through the efforts of two executive directors and many business-savvy board members.

Delta Sigma Phi is a national, not-for-profit social fraternity with a mission of "Building Better Men" for more than a century. Founded in 1899 at the College of the City of New York, "Delta Sig" has grown significantly over the years with 104 active chapters in the United States. Today, the fraternity includes 85,000 living alumni and more than 5,000 undergraduates.

The governance issues faced by Delta Sigma Phi had much to do with the need to update the organizational culture to reflect a changing membership demographic and align with current association practices. It was a long-term, incremental, but fundamental change process. Today's executive director, Patrick Jessee, first served on the board as an undergraduate. He assumed his current role in early 2013. His long-term involvement gave him an excellent vantage point from which to analyze this board.

Challenge: No Growth and No Strategy

There was no obvious or sudden catalyst for Delta Sigma Phi's change. Through the 1990s there had been a number of short-term but ineffective strategic plans. As Jessee put it:

> It was easy to kick the can down the road—we would make markers, not hit them, and then do a new strategic plan. Rebooting every two years and getting nowhere. There was frustration at not being able to create specific intentional growth. We bumped along for a few decades, with no real growth or change.

The fraternity's former executive director, Scott Wiley (now CEO of the Ohio Society of CPAs), came in 2001 at a time when Delta Sigma Phi was getting over some large expenditures. It was the first time critical discussions began to happen about governance, vision, and direction. Wiley observed:

> Our one hundred undergraduate chapters are where the primary activity happens. Chapter self-governance is at the core of the chapter experience: Young college-educated men were exercising personal responsibility and group accountability over their chapter. But that worked against us in creating a stronger national organization.

Jessee added:

> To understand our culture is to understand the broader Greek culture as a whole. It is quite different from other associations. We are not a pay-for-service situation like trade and membership associations are. Ours is built as a bond from an undergraduate experience, focusing on personal ideals and values of that person. Our members have an internal ownership of the organization. A lot more emotion surrounds the perceptions of how we do what

(continued)

(*continued*)

we do, so I think because of that culture you tend to have both potential peril as well as opportunity.

Our leaders are elected by a populace. Our governing board serves *their* emotions and ideals. If that's not properly managed, you can end up where we were prior to this governance phase— a lot of guys who are great members with a lot of passion who can stir a crowd with their perceptions of how to drive values but not necessarily how to drive strategic vision or decision making to reach strategic goals.

A few new board members came in around 2003–2005 and became the change agents. One of the incoming board members had board experience with Price Waterhouse Coopers. Another was owner of a large regional insurance company. The third was an executive in the finance world. A critical mass began to build. They understood business strategic planning and contributed to changing the culture.

Chris Edmonds, past president of the Grand Council (the Fraternity Board), was involved in the transition to a new governance structure. Edmonds began his board tenure in 2005:

I had been a special advisor/observer to this board as a non-elected participant for a number of years prior. I had a great college experience in my chapter. But at the national level there was the lack of long-term vision, lack of strategic plan; it was almost like the inmates running the prison so to speak. We did a strategic plan every five years. It was a long and difficult process. By the time we got the document out, it was about time to start the next planning process. We were great at dreaming but not good at executing.

Strategy: Recruit Change Agents

Edmonds continued:

> Fast forward to 2009. It was a time when we had competing visions of where the organization should go. There was lots of movement on the board. Through Scott's leadership, we finally got the right guys in place who said, "We have to change the model, and the only way to change the model was to have a plan."

Wiley recalled:

> When I became executive director, there was some heavier-than-normal board turnover at the time. In 2003 we hired a consultant, Susan Radwan, to speak to our board. We explored the Policy Governance Model®. Given our recent significant transition in management leadership and board turnover, we found Policy Governance too extreme for us. But the one thing we did like was the notion of a governing board being 100 percent accountable for ensuring an organization's current and future relevancy. And the need to recruit the type of talent a mature governance structure required. And we knew we had a great pool to recruit from; this is one of the strengths of our membership—the diversity of experiences from which to draw.
>
> Today leadership of the organization uses the phrase, "Creating an intentional design," a lot in the boardroom. It's not just an expectation that management will perform and deliver. It's the expectation from members that board members will create a governance structure that will lead us somewhere. Our vision and plan for the future has metrics and measurable outcomes that at any given point allow us to assess where we are and where we are going. We are much more transparent and we know where we are at any moment.

(*continued*)

(continued)

Strategy: Vision *and* Metrics

Edmonds described an important innovation:

We created a strategic plan with a 20-year vision. It's one piece of paper. With a lot of discussion and input from people who cared, we developed a new rallying cry. None of us had joined the "seventh-best" fraternity in the country—in our hearts we joined the *best* fraternity. That became the cultural shift that drove our plan: "What does it mean to be the best?"

The strategic plan was launched at the 2007 convention. Previously we were much like other associations—board members would come as legacy members with pet projects and agendas. But we cut all of that away. And that's when we began to see positive change; it became viral at that point. I credit Scott and his team then, and Patrick and his team since.

> *We created a strategic plan with a 20-year vision. It's one piece of paper.*

Wiley explained:

The governance structure now is very much outcomes-oriented. "Are we deriving the outcomes we envisioned? Are they truly creating a greater level of value for our core constituency?" The board cares about these questions because they have embraced their role as representatives of the owners.

Our governance today has evolved from one of heavy involvement in day-to-day management to a greater level of governance focused on ensuring relevancy, visioning for the future, and creating a system of accountability. The board got to the place where they were able to say to the executive director: "Here are the expectations. You and your team need to come up with an action plan to get that accomplished." The board is now focused on a thriving vision for the future, strategic imperatives around that, and staff responsibility for driving that. We had to embed the idea that national board governance was not like the self-governance of the chapters.

Jessee described a present-day board meeting:

Now every board meeting is focused on the three main pillars of the strategic plan. Our three pillars are developing strong leaders, building stronger chapters, and becoming the strongest fraternity (a few of the metrics include being top five in terms of academics and number one in undergraduate leadership development. Everything focused on the metrics, progress, and the common language of the plan: "This is our purpose as a board: to drive the strategic initiatives of the organization." That helps frame the conversation and avoid derailments of getting into details.

Wiley added:

We also tied it back to our emerging vision to be "best." We weren't there yet, but we were able to begin to articulate how we were working toward that and investing in that so we could be more competitive. This resonated with folks and it became our national tie-in.

Edmonds observed the importance of communicating this message externally:

Today's world is far more complex; our stakeholders are much larger. We are not just competing with others guys on campus. Now we are competing against co-ed organizations on campus. Before, we looked through a prism with a limited view of the world. Things like the parental connection allowed us to broaden that view. Today we get letters from parents who

(continued)

(*continued*)

are thankful that their sons found something bigger than themselves. It all comes back to our focus our message of intentional design. We are better at getting it out there. And "velocity" is something we hear in every one of our board meetings. If you don't have a board addressing a plan, you will have a board full of inertia.

> *"Velocity" is something we hear in every one of our board meetings. If you don't have a board addressing a plan, you will have a board full of inertia.*

Strategy: Good Lines of Communication

The Delta Sigma Phi board used a lot of performance data, ASAE's good governance materials, and board education activities to get the organization where it is today. Now board leaders are talking about consistent board education. They increased their number of board meetings from two to four per year, plus monthly board conference calls. They credit their success especially to an open line of communication between the board chair and executive director. Current executive director Jessee noted:

> I've been fortunate to have two board chairs with whom I have good relationships. A lot of work has to be done at the front end before meetings, discussing touch points, anticipating where conversation could go, ensuring that the chair and I are on same page regarding the goals of meeting. We've done a good job in terms of that. And if things don't go perfectly, I feel empowered to discuss it with the chair.

Strategy: Clarity of Purpose—and Fun

When asked what advice he might pass forward to other association boards, given his broad experience, Wiley, as the former executive director, responded:

First, if you don't have clarity around the direction and the purpose of the organization, these processes are rat holes you are going to continue to go down. At the end of the day, no matter what kind of organization you are, you exist for a purpose.

Second, peer influence is such an important element to effecting any change. When peers are trying to recruit, talking to someone, hearing from others why they are part of something, this can reinforce what is offered by board members and management.

Third, define "What is the trajectory of the organization, what is the relevance and velocity? Do we know where we are going, do we have clarity around our purpose, what that looks like?" This creates that velocity.

Fourth, know why you are recruiting someone and be able to articulate that. It's so easy to get someone on a sinking ship; it's actually harder to get someone aboard a good ship.

And finally, there has to be an element of fun. At the end of the day, people want to be part of something bigger than them, something they can look back on positively and warmly.

Leveraging Internal Momentum to Create Governance Change

Case: American Geophysical Union

 The American Geophysical Union (AGU) was growing and had enormous international credibility. But the board was not governing. Learn how AGU reinvented itself and reconciled "old guard" and "new guard" views of the future.

AGU is an international nonprofit scientific association with more than 60,000 members. Established in 1919 by the National Research Council, AGU operated for 53 years as an un-incorporated affiliate of the National Academy of Sciences, then independently incorporated in 1972.

Unlike some other scientific fields that are far removed from the life of most people, those of AGU members treat processes that influence everyone every day: rainfall rates, trends in marine fisheries, earthquake probabilities, volcanic eruption potentials. We embrace not only the joys of science, but the appreciation of the wondrous mechanisms that make our planet function (Thomas E. Graedel, "AGU Celebrates 80 Years of Leadership, 1919–1999"; http://about.agu.org/our-history/).

Challenge: Growing but Not Governing

To the naked eye, AGU was doing well prior to 2008. It was financially healthy, with an award-winning building and a dedicated and loyal membership. Annual meeting attendance was growing, publications were strong, and upper management was long-tenured and dedicated. The executive director, only the second since AGU's founding, had served for 35 years.

The president-elect at the time, Tim Grove, attended an ASAE program to hear about his responsibilities and came away thinking, "We aren't doing what we are supposed to be doing." So he started asking questions. Volunteer leaders began discussions with the previous executive director about the changes they thought should be taking place, but he was reluctant to change. The board hired a consultant who encouraged them to ask the question, "What would our organization look like today if we were creating it from scratch?" This process led to a leadership transition, and eventually to the hire of Chris McEntee, AGU's executive director.

> *The board hired a consultant who encouraged them to ask the question, "What would our organization look like today if we were creating it from scratch?"*

Strategy: Get an Objective Opinion

Carol Finn, a board officer at the time, described this early work with consultants:

> We invited a visiting committee to come in and review our organization. The basic message was that we were not prepared for the future.
>
> We partnered with Mary Beth Fidler and Cate Bower of Cygnet Strategy; they were critical for us. We knew nothing about current nonprofit organizational and governance best practices. We just knew vaguely that we needed change.
>
> Once our group began working with our consultants, they began to help us understand what we were supposed to do; people really got what was needed. As scientists we know how to fix things. We are able to make quick fact-based decisions. We
>
> *(continued)*

(*continued*)

began to realize that our governance structure had to be different. We had to develop the new process, educate the members about the process, and empower us all to fix the process rather than problems.

We kicked off a future-focused task force to transform us into looking forward. We involved our president, president-elect, and immediate past president.

And I had to have a lot of difficult conversations with people.

We found we had the full support of our council (the board of directors). The desire for change had been so pent up. It seemed hard to justify making changes, because to the outside AGU was seemingly well run. But we found everyone had a story about working with headquarters—it was described as the "black hole"—requests and questions went in but were never responded to.

There was some discomfort with some of the personal aspects of the needed changes, but because people realized it was needed, there was no internal fighting. This was critical; we had pretty much unified our volunteer leadership to support the necessary changes.

Strategy: Team–Building Exercises

Continued Finn:

We launched our strategic planning process at the same time as the staff transition, using a "forum future" process. We did scenario planning and role plays. We had subgroups: strategic planning and governance structure. It was hard work, but it was also fun and engaging. We came up with a new strategic plan and recommendations for a revised governance model that included a new bicameral structure—a board of directors with overall organizational and fiduciary responsibilities and a council to provide scientific direction and that actively involved a much larger science input. It was transparent and well thought out.

The small group responsible for leading the facilitation and implementation of the changes recommended an overlap of members between the old and new governing boards to achieve continuity and cohesion. This was very important. We needed those perspectives to help inform the incoming board that their job was to guide things—not to do the fix but to ensure that the fix gets done. This was a pretty important nuance.

AGU membership approved by 97 percent two major bylaws to revise the governance structure, resulting in a stronger governing board and a representative council. They left the power to approve any future changes to the bylaws with the new council. And then the old council unanimously voted itself out of business to make way for new members.

Cheryl Enderlein, assistant director of leadership, provided Figure 5.1 to describe AGU's new governance structure.

Strategy: A Focus on "Partnership"

Enderlein described a board of 16 members and a council that is "much larger and more interdisciplinary (60–65 people)."

Everyone views their role on the board as a *partnership model* (e.g., partners with staff and volunteers). The board is working quite well. The council is responsible for setting the scientific direction and providing a member perspective to the association. They are

(continued)

(continued)

big and new, and operate with different power than they used to have.

We are still figuring out how to engage all parts of the governance structure and membership groups to most effectively work together. There is still some history and baggage that we are working through. It's still a work in progress.

The chair of every committee or task force is partnered with someone on the staff to ensure that there is equal partnership to fulfill the charge. The roles that committees play at AGU working with the board/council and staff are also clearly defined, as advisors, policy and idea generators, and partners in program implementation, assisting with outreach, speaking, fundraising, communications, and liaisons to members.

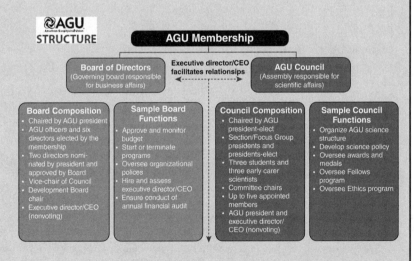

Figure 5.1   AGU Membership Structure
Source: American Geophysical Union.

Strategy: Interim Leadership

Finn added:

Also critical to this change process was the fact that we hired an interim executive director because we knew this was a best practice to follow a longtime-serving staff leader. Our interim executive director was with us for 18 months while we conducted our search process. Our interim helped us provide a credible image for a nonscientist to run the organization. This was important for us to move away from having a scientist. We realized we needed the kind of staff leader to implement the changes we had now agreed on: someone who could help us actualize what we envisioned and who could embrace broadening the decision-making power.

Finn explained: "We wanted a partner. Someone with a collaborative working style and expertise to run a modern nonprofit association. Yet someone who could also represent us well before lawmakers on Capitol Hill."

Chris McEntee, then the newly hired CEO of AGU, recalled:

I have a life-science background and I had run a medical society previously. AGU does more basic discovery than the applied science I came from. So I was familiar with the scientific environment but in a different way.

It was a unique experience to come into a situation where they had already done so much heavy lifting and my role was to implement these changes. They had already made a lot of decisions about new ways of doing things. Much was already on paper as approved.

(continued)

(*continued*)

At our first board meeting under the new governance model, we invited governance expert Nancy Axelrod. She focused on, "Now you've put this all on paper, but what does this mean for how you want to act and work?" That meeting was critical. We were still in a somewhat fragile place. You can easily fall into old habits of doing things, so we spent a lot of time at that first meeting of the board going over the documents and asking ourselves, "What does this really mean?"

Nancy's approach was perfect for AGU: "What kind of organization are you and what do you want to be?" They came out 60 percent on strategic, 30 percent on "nose-in, fingers-out oversight," and 10 percent on their own development as a board, about learning about how to govern well and becoming knowledgeable about topics to govern AGU well.

We came up with a two-year board and council work plan. For both governing groups, the work plan outlined the major issues they would discuss over a two-year period. We work hard to be knowledge based and strategic, with appropriate oversight.

For all of our meetings, including committees and task forces, our agenda always has the type of discussion needed (strategic, operational oversight, development issue), whether a decision is expected, and how does each link to our strategic plan. We have a structure and a process and policy, but we don't have a lot of hard and fast rules, and that allows us to be flexible and nimble. We try to steer away from set rules.

[A sample of an AGU agenda illustrates the association's focus on strategies and outcomes (see Figure 5.2).]

AGU worked hard on coming up with a structure for the delegation of the authority for decision making. McEntee described the process:

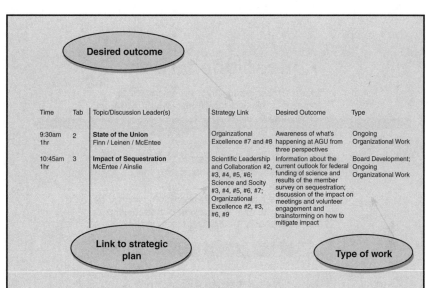

Figure 5.2   AGU Strategies and Outcomes
Source: American Geophysical Union.

Our authority matrix and decision tree has been critical to
our process. They lead to additional policies like AGU's organizational relationship policy. If the relationship is low-risk,
requires small dollars, and is consistent with our strategic plan
and values, then staff can make the decision. If it is high-risk,
high-dollars, we involve internal and external expertise as
needed. Who makes the decision is far less important than the
quality of information and insight on which the decision is made.
All groups—board, council, committees, and staff—are regularly
asking themselves four key questions (see Figures 5.3 and 5.4).

(continued)

(continued)

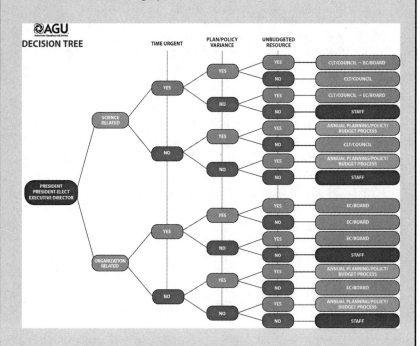

4 questions to ask...

1. What member perspectives are important to consider in this decision (career stage, discipline, US vs. not US, etc.?)
2. How do we think members might react if they were present in this discussion?
3. What other stakeholder perspectives/viewpoints are important to consider in making this decision?
4. If members could voice their opinion, would they think this was well aligned with our strategic plan and what priority would they place on this?

Figure 5.3 Four Key Questions

Source: American Geophysical Union.

Figure 5.4 AGU Decision Tree

Source: American Geophysical Union.

AGU's new governance committee also plays a critical role in board-building. McEntee recalled:

We thought through this very carefully. It is chaired by the past president of the board with an additional three appointments from the board and three appointments from the council. When identifying future candidates for leadership, they look for diverse perspectives, representing the entire organization, a given. Then they look for people with leadership skills such as how to work in a collective, and those who can disagree without being disagreeable. And then they plan the formal orientation for incoming volunteer leaders.

Enderlein added:

Through our governance committee process, we get the best outcomes because we demonstrate to the candidates what kind of organization we are. We are training them from the very first interaction. This is our opportunity. We have to deepen our leadership pool and can best do that by pushing down to provide more education and training not only into our council, but also in member groups, committees, task forces, and so on. All this works together in order for us to have volunteer leaders who understand more completely our culture and our organization.

Today, AGU is a knowledge-based organization with clear and focused strategies and defined roles and responsibilities. Board members consider themselves flexible and nimble with the ability to take on big decisions. At all levels, the organization has implemented improved processes and tools for organizational work. As a final example of internal tools used, AGU usesFigure 5.5 with volunteer leaders as they take on decision-making work.

(continued)

(continued)

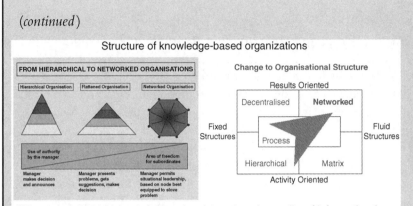

"Who makes the decision is far less important than the quality of information & insight on which the decision is made."

Figure 5.5   Structure of Knowledge-Based Organizations
Source: American Geophysical Union.

Finn, Enderlein, and McEntee shared the lessons AGU learned, which may be of value to other associations:

- Heed the warning signs.
- Engage the members in the discussion.
- Change the model—*and the work.*
- Gain clarity on roles and responsibilities.
- Trust the process.
- Establish a culture that gives people the benefit of the doubt.
- Communicate in effective ways.
- Be patient! It takes time to coordinate change across the organization and bring people along.
- Evaluate as you go and adjust as needed. Flexibility is key.

6

Leading Up
The CEO's Opportunity

A leader is one who knows the way, goes the way, and shows the way.
—John C. Maxwell, author, speaker, and pastor

As the preceding case of the American Geophysical Union illustrated, a healthy partnership between CEO and board members is one of the ingredients for successful board change. The best partnerships are those in which the CEO facilitates a more strategic board. Chris McEntee, AGU's executive director (ED), described her responsibility to the board:

> From my perspective it is really important for me to think through how I can best put the background information to make it come alive for discussion and decision making. The processes and systems needed to fulfill what you really mean by strategic governance. This does start with a partnership with the board chair in creating the agendas and with the staff and pulling together the necessary background for agenda items.

139

CEO-led board change sounds odd or perhaps vaguely threatening, except to those who have experienced it. Some people believe a board has the fiduciary duty to lead itself. However, nonprofit research clearly suggests that such normative ideas of governance, emphasizing the board's unequivocal leadership role, create unrealistic expectations for boards (Heimovics and Herman 1990; Jäger and Rehli 2012; Miller-Millesen 2003; Stone and Ostrower 2007).

Rather than consider CEO action to improve the governance model a "failure" of the board, it is better to accept it as a common and realistic situation for many associations. Often CEOs have more information—and perhaps more management training—than the board chair or the board as a whole and will see a need for change earlier and more quickly than others simply by virtue of their place in the organization. And sometimes the timely need for change or improvement can be at odds with the ability to work on these given the constraints of volunteer time and board meeting schedules. CEO-led change also occurs because the repercussions of a weak board fall most heavily on staff. Therefore, the "psychological centrality" of the CEO to organizational success cannot be denied (Heimovics and Herman 1990, p. 70).

CEO-led change does not happen in a vacuum, however. In a case that follows this chapter, Susan Keating, president and CEO of the National Foundation for Credit Counseling, played a crucial role in leading a major governance change process. Keating observed the need for stakeholder involvement in the process at all levels of the organization, as well as the importance of listening to critics and having the courage to compromise. And many of our interview subjects also observed the need for the board to *trust* the CEO through a change process.

Concepts and Application

Boards that embrace rather than feel threatened by staff-initiated change do a great service to themselves and their organizations.

They also reduce their risk of losing good staff. But most importantly, many experts suggest the strongest organizations are built on principles of complementary partnership between the CEO and board (Chait, Ryan, and Taylor 2005; Cornforth 2012; Harris 1993). As Williams and McGinnis (2007, p. ix) explain:

> The qualities of a true partnership—support, trust, honesty, forth-rightness, respect, and understanding—must belong to both the chief executive and the board. Just like building any relationship, the process calls for hard work by both parties. But the rewards, including success for the organization and the chief executive, are worth the effort.

When a CEO is "leading up," the activity is often not the direct influencing of action but rather recognizing that a specific change is needed and then building the necessary consciousness-raising with key players in an organization. While at times a CEO will be a governance group facilitator, there are also times when a CEO has the opportunity to lead from behind the scenes. "Leading up" does not mean "controlling up" or even "managing up." Primarily it means establishing one's position to be trusted so that one can have appropriate influence (for example, in the words of one interviewee, building up "social capital"). Over and over, the CEOs and executive directors whom we interviewed observed that successful board change occurred only after the staff had earned the board's trust.

> "Leading up is the act of working with people above you—whether one boss, several bosses, a chief executive, a board of directors . . . to help them and you get a better job done. Organizations need more overall direction from below to think strategically, communicate persuasively, and act decisively" (Useem 2001).

As a chief executive, to establish trust means to show evidence to your board chair and your board that you act with integrity. You say what you mean and you mean what you say; your words and comments are respectful and positive at all times. You follow through on your commitments and you demonstrate your ability to make things happen; you can be counted on to provide value. Other qualities that are needed to successfully lead up (as well as lead sideways and down) are showing initiative that benefits all, handling the hard stuff in addition to the easy stuff, being prepared and facilitating the preparedness for others, knowing which battles to take on and which to let go, sharing the limelight, and helping others to look good. Individuals who work on personal growth for themselves are often those who earn the trust of others and who are influencers. As you will see in the case of the Northwest Association of Independent Schools later in this chapter, its former executive director, Meade Thayer, often invoked two mantras to nudge thoughtful change dialogue: "Does this rise to the level of governance?" and "Help me understand."

The board–chief executive relationship is about personal dynamics. No one enjoys conflict or confrontation, especially with regard to a professional colleague. As we have observed in Chapter 5, successfully working in a group context is highly dynamic and can engender great passion and emotion when disagreements or conflicts erupt. Paying attention to these dynamics and actively honoring the human element requires commitment and work (Kissman 2009). One way to make that happen is to involve key professional staff in some of the board's team-building activities. As the athlete Michael Jordan once said, "Talent wins games, but teamwork and intelligence win championships."

In another case that follows this chapter, Mary Bayat, the 2014 chair-elect of the Northern Virginia Association of REALTORS®, observed:

A lot of [our success] is a credit to how our CEO works with the board. She promotes good dialogue. We have a lot of gatherings to talk to each other if we see problems. She is not afraid and she helps us think ahead. The board identifies needs in our profession, the staff comes up with great ideas, the board discusses them, and we come up with great solutions.

Summary

Nothing is more critical to the success of an organization than a positive and constructive relationship between the board and its paid staff leader. While at times one may be out in front of the other, true and effective change leading to transformational governance change or governance high performance requires mutual trust and respect through teamwork between these two partners.

The three cases that follow this chapter demonstrate association boards that had the vision to seek not only new expertise through a CEO hire but also a real change agent who was able, through the trust built by a track record of success in one area, to help orchestrate a complete governance change.

Leading Change with a Constructive Board–CEO Partnership

Case: The Northern Virginia Association of REALTORS®

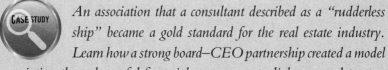 *An association that a consultant described as a "rudderless ship" became a gold standard for the real estate industry. Learn how a strong board–CEO partnership created a model association through careful financial management, dialogue, and trust.*

The Northern Virginia Association of REALTORS® (NVAR) was established in 1921 with about 40 members. Today it has grown to more than 10,000 real estate agents who

(continued)

(*continued*)

collectively transact $11 billion of housing sales in a community of more than 2 million residents. NVAR belongs to a network of hundreds of local and state associations that comprise the National Association of REALTORS® (NAR; nvar.com/about-nvar/about-nvar/about-nvar-mission-statement).

Christine M. Todd, CAE, chief executive officer, came to NVAR in 1989. When she became the CEO, she brought two characteristics somewhat in short supply in an association in need of diversification: She was young and female. Her appointment was high profile and she broke that glass ceiling.

Challenge: A Rudderless Ship, Taking on Water

Fortunately for Todd, two years earlier, the board president at the time, Pam McCoach, had already realized the association needed diversifying and had begun to tap a new generation of men and women with the help of other board members. She persuaded the board to conduct a structural audit led by a consultant, Jim Ferguson. Todd recalls:

> Ferguson was asked, "We think the association is broken in so many places but we don't know where to start." The board knew there was something wrong but didn't know what. It took about four months to conduct the structural audit. Jim brought in four or five other experts in the process. His delivery of a 20-page report to the board took four hours. [The news] was not good. He used the analogy that NVAR was like a rudderless ship; like an ocean liner where on the top deck everything looked fine, but below, the infrastructure was in decay—it was actually listing and taking on water. And the ship was being run aground.

Challenge: Wrong CEO for the Job

The board was devastated by the report. This was not easy news to swallow. Nor were Ferguson's recommendations, with the first that NVAR hire a new CEO with management experience immediately. Todd described the events leading up to her hire:

> Someone on the board said, "Well, we've had our CEO for seven years. Whom else could we possibly get?" There was an angry exchange, but Ferguson said, "You can turn this ship around if you put the right person in the job." The board got silent, and then passed a resolution to replace the CEO.

Challenge: Weak Infrastructure

The events leading to this crisis point were gradual but cumulative. In the 1980s, membership was growing because the housing market was good, but NVAR's infrastructure was weak. The software to manage the budget was inadequate. Committee members were loose about recording accurate minutes and on follow-through of decisions. The organization had not had a financial audit in three years. Todd explained the impact:

> We had plenty of money, but its mismanagement actually made us financially unstable. We had to get the fiscal house in order. And because the board was so focused on balancing the budget, they couldn't focus on membership growth and legislative advocacy. The membership didn't realize how bad it was, but the leadership did. Board members could see chaos, but the staff could not. Membership tolerated it because they had an overly
>
> *(continued)*

(continued)

friendly CEO who ran things like a social club. No one wanted to say, "Something's wrong."

Strategy: Reestablish Board Trust in Staff

With the departure of the old CEO and Christine Todd's hire, the board and new CEO embarked on the hard work leading change that had to happen.

It was unbelievable how involved and exhausted they were, and how off track the association had become. While they said to me, "You are our future, we trust you; we will do whatever you say to help you turn this ship around," it took them a long time to truly trust me and other staff and volunteers in the initial upheaval. The good news for me as the incoming executive was that I did not have to deliver bad news; they had already heard it from an expert. But the bad news was how difficult it was in the beginning. I also had to reestablish trust and confidence between the leadership and the staff, to get everyone to row together. It took three years to slowly build the board confidence in the staff so the board would not be in the weeds and could assume a more strategic role.

When I came, I took away cocktail parties and expense accounts. We separated the finance committee from the board. I also told the board that I would need the financial and the human resources to do what needed to be done. They allowed me to rebuild the staff. They said, "Whatever you need—the only way to go is up."

Strategy: Make Good Use of Volunteers

Our biggest asset was very dedicated and focused volunteers. They are what made the journey from chaotic to what is now beautifully managed and run. It was a team effort. We had a dedicated volunteer leadership who understood and respected the role of the CEO and allowed me to do what I needed to do.

NVAR used outside consulting help for more than a year; the entire overhaul took five years. Today NVAR is considered the gold standard. The association has been used as a model and has helped other REALTOR® associations nationally and internationally to achieve high performance by strengthening their governance and organizational operations.

Mary Bayat, 2014 chair-elect, had been in the industry for 28 years and involved with the board since 2003. She recalled:

Today our board is one of the most powerful in the area and the nation in our industry. I remember the tremendous change. A lot of this is a credit to how Chris works with the board and we have a really great staff that works like clockwork. We are all really professional. Chris promotes good dialogue. We have a lot of gatherings to talk to each other if we see problems. Chris is not afraid and she helps us think ahead. The board identifies needs in our profession; Chris and the staff come up with great ideas, the board discusses them, and we come up with great solutions. For example, we are way ahead of our time with technology. Every year we are moving ahead.

Challenge: Board Demographics Don't Represent Membership

A big part of all these changes came from the growing recognition that the industry was changing. Todd observed:

About 1998, it was clear that the demographics in our industry were changing dramatically and our board was not reflective of the profile of who was in our business. Election of 21 board

(continued)

(continued)

members with 30–40 people running was a popularity contest. Our governance structure was broken. I realized I was not getting the best and the brightest on the board. I went back to the board and posed the question: "How can we better reflect the profile of the membership?" For example, our membership is ethnically diverse, but all board members were older, white, and from the residential side of our business. I said, "We cannot be successful if you stay exclusively within an ethnic group." So we had to change the voting structure.

Strategy: Make Board Selection Serve Diversity Needs

Continued Todd:

I recommended that we elect our leadership in an entirely different way. Previously only 10 percent of our members voted in an election. Usually there were only about six people running for election. It was a popularity contest and it was abusing the system.

Today NVAR has a fully functioning nominating committee. The association eliminated "bullet" voting (i.e., a predetermined list of candidates developed through a self- or other nomination process voted on by a membership typically online or through snail mail or at an annual meeting) and have changed it to a hybrid between membership elections (based on vetted recommendations) and self-perpetuating appointments.

After the election, the new chair looks at the pool of those who were not elected as well as outside the pool and appoints three additional at-large members. The caveat to these appointments was that these individuals had to bring something extra to the board composition—a needed "fresh lens of perspective" such as cultural diversity or industry representation to make sure that all the real estate disciplines were represented on the board and to reflect the profile of the Northern Virginia membership overall. These chair-appointed individuals serve for one year, a decision also designed to create a greater lens of diversity. Todd described the results:

> We are now down to 16 board members. This new structure became valued and appreciated throughout the membership. It changed the complexion of the board entirely and everyone felt more included.

A smaller board not only meant that nominations had to be carefully managed to achieve representative goals. NVAR also decided to create membership forums and special-interest groups to engage members in topical areas of interest. Out of these forums come its future leaders. Chair-elect Bayat explained:

> This gave us a chance to provide more meaningful member engagement and representation. At every gathering we look at our members and we follow up with those who demonstrate some expertise that would be advantageous to us. We are always looking for new leaders and not recycling old leaders. This is how we stay on top of the issues.

Other small but important governance changes included reemphasizing the board's fiduciary duty of care. The association instituted a procedure to provide the board materials in advance and ensure that they were read ahead of the meeting. They practiced agenda management to keep meetings focused and to the point.

NVAR also uses deliberate board development strategies. It actively identifies and trains potential board members in a
(continued)

(*continued*)

custom-designed Leadership Institute that taps into the Northern Virginia REALTOR® Institute and the Virginia Association
of REALTORS® Leadership Academy. The purpose of these
efforts is not just to present governance needs but to plant seeds
for future leadership with personality tests, team building,
leadership training. The National Association of REALTORS®
also conducts a leadership program for incoming board chairs in
which CEOs participate.

Moving forward on such a positive governance platform has
led to many other organizational changes, all embraced by the
board and membership. Todd recalled:

> The scary part is that you'd better deliver when the board puts
> that much trust in you. I was so thankful the board was so very
> supportive because I was worried that I was always giving them
> bad news. So at the end of the year at one of our conventions
> we made it really fun-filled. And the board at the time said,
> "Chris, we needed this so badly." This was a huge lesson for
> me—give them a break, have fun. We work hard and we play
> hard (appropriately!). We find a good balance. I now take full
> advantage of the opportunities when we have everyone together.
>
> Now that I am more mature, with lots of successes under my
> belt, I have a lot more respect with the board. I also understand
> when to pick and choose my battles. I use the board and
> volunteer leadership as "content experts." The issues that are
> their bailiwick, their livelihood, I back off on. The issues that are
> critically important for the organization, I fight. We really are
> one big happy family. But when we have to make hard decisions
> we will do so.

An Incoming CEO Gets Governance Change in Motion

Case: National Foundation for Credit Counseling

 This is a remarkable story of changing governance from a representative board to a hybrid board led by an incoming CEO. As many representational associations often note the problems with having a constituency-based board, this case shows how one organization managed to work with reluctant members to achieve the best of both worlds.

As the nation's largest financial counseling organization, the National Foundation for Credit Counseling (NFCC) is a Member Agency Network including more than 600 community-based offices located in all 50 states and Puerto Rico. NFCC Member Agencies and their NFCC-certified financial counselors provide financial counseling and education to millions of consumers each year in person, over the phone, or online (www.nfcc.org).

NFCC was founded in 1951. As of 2014, this 501(c)3 had 83 organizational members. Its journey toward high performance stemmed from external impacts that required the organization to look at its governance practices differently in the context of current and anticipated future realities.

Challenge: Competition and Lack of Differentiation

Susan C. Keating was recruited as the president and CEO of NFCC in March 2004. She had spent 29 years in financial services as a major player. She recalled:

(*continued*)

(continued)

At the time of my recruitment, the NFCC was reeling from a very difficult environment. New entrants into the sector increased competition overall, and alarmingly some were targeting some of the most vulnerable consumers with predatory and abusive practices. I was hired by the NFCC board to turn things around and to differentiate the NFCC from others by working with the federal government and other stakeholders. At this time, I and several NFCC members worked with Congressional staff members and participated directly in hearings. The NFCC was formally acknowledged as the "gold standard of the industry" and the federal government and private sector supported the need for new and better practices to serve the public.

Keating's keen understanding of the industry and her previous relationships provided her with a strong sphere of influence. Additionally, she put a great team in place at the NFCC to drive the changes.

Challenge: Board Lacks Broad Expertise

Once the organization got through this critical phase, Keating became aware that to move NFCC to the next level, a "bold and innovative new governance model" was needed—one that would tap the perspectives of leaders from a variety of disciplines to reshape the NFCC's outlook and ensure sustainability. NFCC needed to expand its capacity to meet future challenges but also retain the critical elements of membership control over internal matters. Keating explained how she got the conversation started:

I introduced to our member-based board the idea that a broader lens was needed and new strategies were needed. But while this was my vision, the path to get there was not as clear. To move us forward the NFCC conducted a membership survey that provided input for new Core Strategies. One of these became: *Core Strategy #10: Develop a proposed board profile and plan to fill and transition to the desired board profile.*

Strategy: Get External Expertise

Our next step involved engaging a senior governance consultant with BoardSource, Katha Kissman, and at the initial client intake conversation that took place in December 2006, I remember thinking, "We really need to do this."

Strategy: Research Governance Best Practices

The first steps in that client engagement process included:

- Research on governance in similar membership organizations
- Interviews with the CEO, the general counsel, and other board members to further understand the existing structure and its strengths and weaknesses
- A survey of members to understand the issues and plant the seeds for a vision for change
- A whitepaper that analyzed the present state and future possibilities of the board

The initial findings as reported at a January 2007 NFCC Governance Task Force Meeting, chaired by Suzanne Boas, showed data about nonprofit organizations that had completed a board transition from one kind of board structure to another. In this report, organizations such as Amnesty International USA, the Sierra Club, the Lupus Foundation, and Hostelling International were used as examples of boards that had changed

(continued)

(*continued*)

their governance to new structures that had not previously existed. The most common considerations for these organizations were:

- Determining and forming a clear articulation for why the change better served an organization's needs and goals
- The importance of building understanding and support for any proposed change with the membership
- Involving the membership in the transition process
- Open and transparent governance
- Keeping a structured mechanism for a two-way communication process between the membership and the board

In some cases, the transition was done in phases. Keating described her board's reaction:

After presentation of the survey results and the initial findings, the board discussed with the task force concerns about moving the organization to a new governance structure and the pros and cons of alternative structures such as a hybrid or self-perpetuating board. We addressed likely member-based decision issues and identified key skills and gaps needed within the board to achieve the new vision.

Strategy: Engage with the Critics

We convened a study group and pulled together the most ardent critics. My theory was if we put bright people together and presented them with the same information, then we would find common ground.

Meetings and phone discussions led up to a planned presentation to the membership at the NFCC Spring Meeting in April 2007, followed by a plan to present new bylaws at the NFCC Annual Meeting in October 2007. But the first effort to change the bylaws narrowly failed. Keating described next steps:

> The members' biggest fear was that the outside entities would take control and change the mission, potentially changing the model for services the NFCC has provided for decades. But a critical core group of members supported the changes. So we convened a study group and pulled together the most ardent critics. My theory was if we put bright people together and presented them with the same information, then we would find common ground. There was clearly an opportunity and a need for the NFCC membership to play a larger role in finding a better structure.

Strategy: Align Board's Profile with New Strategic Needs

In June 2009, Keating convened a small, diverse, and representative group of NFCC leaders, including representatives who actively opposed the 2008 initiative, to study the alignment of the NFCC's board profile with the organization's priorities.

> The study group met over the course of the next year. After extensive discussion there was unanimous support for the notion that "we need to match our board profile with the new world around us." The study group concluded and recommended recruitment of individuals with strong professional experience, a particular knowledge base, and leadership that was not represented in the organization at the time.

The membership was consulted and a new idea emerged to provide the best of both worlds:

(continued)

(continued)

[A] board with experts to provide a wealth of strategic thinking and decision making tempered by the real-world experience of an array of agencies; and an operating committee, representing member interests and issues which had the expertise and control over internal and operational matters that would otherwise distract and consume the limited time resources of the board.

Source: Internal NFCC document.

Through communications, discussion, and ongoing education, support for the changes to the bylaws was built, and at the NFCC Annual Meeting in 2009, NFCC members approved a completely new governance structure with the creation of two entities: a new board of trustees and an operating committee. The NFCC membership approved the changes by an 83 percent vote.

Strategy: Ambitious Recruitment

The current composition of the 15-member board was built through a complicated process honoring those areas NFCC felt needed more reach, experience, and influence. Through a formal nominating committee, they identified specific categories such as education, communications, housing, legal, financial services, economists, and so on, posing the question: "If we all could pick our very first choices, who would be our candidates for the board?" An external consultant, Tim McNamara, Boyden and Associates, led the conversation on board qualities and criteria, and then the search. Keating described the successful outcome:

Depending upon who knew whom, we conducted some outreach and then Cathy Allen of the Santa Fe Group and I did the actual recruiting. Only one person turned us down because he didn't have time, and that was Colin Powell. We were amazed—to a person, they said yes. This was right in the middle of the financial crisis and suddenly the NFCC's mission and work were very aligned with the national interest in financial responsibility and financial literacy. The board candidates to whom we reached out wanted to be part of the solution during a very troubled time.

Today, three years beyond the bylaws changes, the individuals recruited for the at-large positions are still in partnership with the seven member-elected representative positions, who provide a needed member perspective. Today, said Keating:

We are operating quite well. The guidance and thought leadership of the new at-large board members helped the membership serve more consumers during the financial crisis and helped the NFCC through some financial challenges. Some additional changes may be needed over time, however. For example, I almost have two separate boards, so I often serve two masters, which can be time consuming and challenging. However, we found what works for us during an important time in our history and it became a member-sanctioned solution. The time and energy to get where we are today was worth the investment.

A Board Puts Its Trust in an Association Professional

Case—Northwest Association of Independent Schools

 A supportive and respectful executive–board collaboration, driven by association know-how and the mantra, "Does this rise to the level of governance?" allowed this too-operational board to create a governance structure the organization could grow with.

The Northwest Association of Independent Schools (NWAIS) covers eight states and supports 110 schools. The Association guides, inspires, and advances schools through accreditation, workshops, and resource sharing, and by fostering collegial relationships and ethical leadership (www.nwais.org/page.cfm?p=449).

Challenge: Operational Board

Meade Thayer, just recently retired as the executive director, and Rob Camner, former board chair and a current board member with 12 years on the board, were instrumental in the changes that occurred to bring NWAIS into greater governance and organizational performance. According to Thayer, throughout the mid-1980s and 1990s, an overly large board accustomed to running the association had transitioned to paid staff, which resulted in less oversight. However, with a new ED coming in, there was a desire to be more involved with the crafting of new initiatives. Arriving in 1998, Thayer brought a résumé combining prior independent school credentials and association management expertise:

In independent school associations, there are very few leaders who come from the association world. We come from working in our schools. Working with our board, I helped them understand that as the board of the NWAIS they were not running their school but an association. As Dick Chait stated, they were acting like a huddle of quarterbacks. There began fledgling understanding and awareness of the need to improve.

Camner recalled:

We were becoming larger. We recognized that the governance structure needed to change to be effective. In a typical nonprofit, board members are drawn from a wide range of life experience. In ours, we were all very operationally oriented. So we had to step back and allow our management to do that. We weren't running the organization. For us, the question became: "Does this rise to the level of governance?"

Strategy: Ask Good Questions about Board's Role

Thayer added:

My style coming in was to say, "Help me understand." For example, in my earlier years, whenever a new school wanted

> *Does this rise to the level of governance?*

to join NWAIS, I had to take a board member with me to vet their membership. It was collegial, but fundamentally this was an operational issue. We worked hard to evaluate why it was felt the board had to do this, and as they gained more faith in me as executive director and had a greater understanding of respective

(continued)

(*continued*)

roles and responsibilities, we revised the membership approval process. By the time I left, new school membership applications were evaluated and approved solely by me [with an FYI to the board]. It was a combination of more faith in me as an executive director as well as the board shifting from an operational to a strategic focus.

Strategy: Shift Responsibilities as Trust Grows

Camner continued:

Many other changes related to trust. When Meade joined us he had not been a head of school. So we didn't know exactly what we could expect. We concluded that capacity as an association leader rather than having been a head of school was appropriate for where we were organizationally. And we have been able to adopt other changes as our trust in Meade grew.

With these changes also came a shifting of responsibilities. The full membership now only votes on changes to mission, bylaws, and new trustees. Business meetings that were up to six hours long are now an hour long, with the rest of the time used for professional development.

Strategy: Clarify Mission to Clarify Board Role

Thayer described another strategy he used:

I also said "help me understand" with regard to the mission. Before, we were there to help all schools. So we worked to define what we meant by *all schools*. This has been a long, ongoing, and evolving conversation that has clarified with which types of schools we were willing to work. Now we are here to strengthen independent schools in the region.

Camner explained how accreditation standards shape the association's role:

Some associations are open to anyone in the field who pays the dues. There's no need for standards for membership in an organization of that kind. But [with standards] our big questions were: What kinds of schools do we wish to serve? What do we have to have in common to be members? This became a more profound conversation than I've had in other membership organizations.

Thayer continued:

Another big area for dialogue was around the stated importance of "free and open inquiry." While everyone talked about it and believed in it, there was no articulation of what that meant in any organizational document when I first arrived.

But Thayer notes that it is now one of the association's core values and included in accreditation standards.

We also looked at financial stability. This financial difficulty was a trigger point for the board to start asking the right kinds of governance questions: How do we raise revenues? How do we strengthen financial controls? Do we have the right accreditation process? What about a commitment to diversity? Then we spent the next couple of years exploring our core values.

(continued)

(continued)

Strategy: Nimbleness through Task Forces

Thayer described how the board's culture shifted to becoming more intentional about its own purpose:

Rob's challenge to the board (as chair) was, "If we are going to be an association of independent schools and hold them to accreditation practices, we needed to be a model board." We learned a lot from ASAE and BoardSource. For example, Rob also posed the question: "What does it mean to get away from standing committees, instead using task forces?" We developed official charges and annual work plans for our standing committees. And we got very good at using task forces.

Camner elaborated on the decision to invest in task forces:

We got very good at using task forces. Anything that's difficult . . . can't have a robust conversation in a group of 18 people.

Anything that's difficult or challenging can't have a robust conversation in a group of 18 people—there are too many people around the table. Sometimes we used task forces for recommendations, sometimes for just defining the important questions to inform a board-level conversation later.

Strategy: Involve Not Just Current but Potential Stakeholders

The new governance focus allowed the board to take on some major initiatives, including creating detailed accreditation standards for current and aspiring member schools that helped to increase membership. Thayer explained:

No other association of independent schools that accredits is currently recognizing the needs of schools in the developmental stages. One of the greatest governance *aha* moments for us was having a nonmember ("subscriber") school involved in the planning. It was very helpful to see what we were doing from their lens and led us to realize: "How we can build our future board unless we involve people along the way?"

Strategy: Clarify Decision-Making Roles

To guide future decision making, NWAIS board and staff borrowed a document from the National Association of Independent Schools, the "Design of the Partnership—Board/Head" decision model with an accompanying exercise used in the boardroom and in board orientation. The model in Figure 6.1 offers board members a useful reminder about roles and helps them stay focused on strategic issues. This diagram is also used in board trainings for member schools. Thayer observed that its real benefit is in the conversations that the board and executive director/Head have about what rises up to the level of strategy, what is a partnership, and what is operational. These conversations help establish precedents for future board action and future executive director/Head action.

(continued)

(continued)

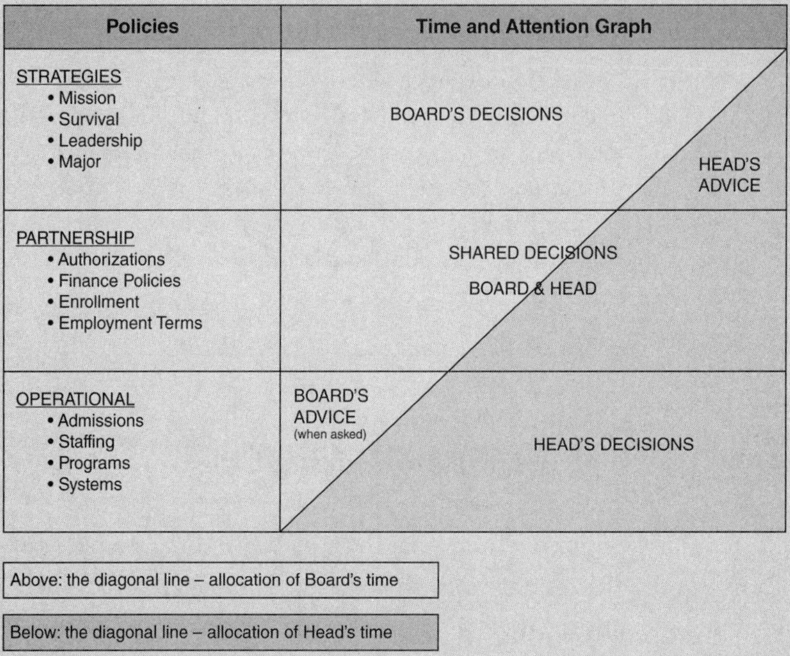

Policies	Time and Attention Graph
STRATEGIES • Mission • Survival • Leadership • Major	BOARD'S DECISIONS HEAD'S ADVICE
PARTNERSHIP • Authorizations • Finance Policies • Enrollment • Employment Terms	SHARED DECISIONS BOARD & HEAD
OPERATIONAL • Admissions • Staffing • Programs • Systems	BOARD'S ADVICE (when asked) HEAD'S DECISIONS

Above: the diagonal line – allocation of Board's time

Below: the diagonal line – allocation of Head's time

Figure 6.1 Design of the Partnership—Board/Head
Source: From the *NAIS Trustee Handbook*, Fifth Edition.

Strategy: Nimble Bylaws

Thayer described the outcome:

> While NWAIS has come a long way, the changes have been a gradual process. We've changed our bylaws five or six times during my tenure. But they had always been broad, never overly prescribed. Rob always said the more specific they are, the more likelihood you will violate them.

Camner explained:

In my view, bylaws are supposed to be like the U.S. Constitution. There's a reason why the Constitution hasn't been amended very much over the last 200-plus years. It was very deliberately not intended to be an operations manual.

(See bylaws at www.nwais .org/uploaded/files/ Nov2013_NWAIS_Bylaws .pdf.)

Bylaws are supposed to be like the U.S. Constitution. . . . The Constitution is not an operations manual.

7 | Leading Forward
The Board Chair's Opportunity

The master doesn't talk, he acts. When his work is done, the people say 'Amazing! We did it all by ourselves.'

—Lao-Tzu, philosopher and poet

The CEO of the American Camp Association, Peg L. Smith, had been with the organization for 10 years when the deep changes started to take place. Peg developed and presented a passionate "call to action," a three-page document that challenged the board to think in a completely fundamental and revolutionary way. As Peg recalls:

> I had worked with ACA for a decade. The board had great vision and dreams and opportunity but was very insular, made up of people from the field. They wanted to be more external and have greater relevance to the broader community, but they just couldn't make it happen. The board had always been putting the staff in the situation of hearing all their big dreams for the organization that couldn't

possibly be realized with the conditions the way they were. It was not fair and we weren't going anywhere.

Over the previous five years, we had been through a name change and a rebranding. We did everything on the surface to look different, but inside we weren't different. We had done all the buffing and polishing that we could and I knew we had to go to the next step to really make change. My "call to action" was about working as one association. It wasn't detailed; there was much ambiguity. My intention was to invite the board to look at the road to the vision as an opportunity and a journey. We knew where we wanted to get to, but we had to create the road as we went.

In retrospect, I now see that I had two incredible things that made what happened next happen. First, I had built a good deal of social capital and trust within the organization to allow me to voice the need for this next critical step. And second, I knew that we had a board president at the time who had the right competency, attitude, and credibility in our organization to lead.

The board chair, separately or in conjunction with the chief executive, is in a prime position to ascertain needed change and, without a doubt, is the person who *must* lead governance change. While a CEO will play a critical role in the development and implementation of any plan for governance change (unless the change is *about* the CEO), the process cannot be led by a CEO. Peer-to-peer leadership is critical, and the board chair will engage other board members to take ownership for the change and actively find ways to involve them in the process.

Board chairs are unlikely to succeed at leading change unless they have a clear understanding of their role, the skills to implement it, and the trust of the full board. The chair's responsibility to not only *preside* over meetings but to *facilitate* a successful board dynamic can easily get overlooked in the busyness of mastering agenda management and Robert's Rules. Little nonprofit research exists to guide board leadership. However, the governance literature is firm about "the board chair's obligation to stakeholders . . . to facilitate the work of the board in the context of effective leadership and good governance" (Wertheimer 2008). As Smith of American Camp Association recalled about her board chair, Ann Sheets:

There are moments when you really doubt what you have started. But if not for Ann's leadership, the volunteer board members would not have been able to get through the messiness. When you have leadership that publicly appears resolute and committed to a vision, that's inspiring and it allows change to unfold. Ann was always inspirational and enthusiastic about what the changes would ultimately mean. The initial courage and commitment and willingness to embrace chaos happened under Ann's leadership.

Concepts and Application

Group Facilitation Skills

The board chair's ability to support effective group dynamics during organizational change can mean the difference between successful board member retention (if that is the goal) and wholesale desertion. Wertheimer's (2008, p. 26) *Board Chair Handbook* wisely includes material on a range of team management and interpersonal skills, such as:

One-on-one communication skills—listening, question formulation, probing for shared meaning, empathy, and confrontation— become the foundation for group facilitation skills. For a board chair, the challenge is to apply these skills in dialogue with a group of individuals. As a group facilitator, you must show attentiveness, responsiveness, and flexibility toward the group process and, at the same time, acknowledge and respond to individual comments—all while respecting the allotted time and focusing on the task at hand. It requires skill to direct participants' comments to remain on task and to help clarify and summarize points that others are making.

Board chairs should not assume they have the natural skills or experience for effective group facilitation. They may find training and resources on effective group facilitation helpful, such as Schwarz et al.'s (2005, p. 3) values-based set of group facilitation objectives, outlined briefly here:

1. Increase the quality of decisions.
2. Increase commitment to decision.
3. Reduce effective implementation time.
4. Improve working relationships.
5. Improve personal satisfaction in groups.
6. Increase organizational learning.

Generative Thinking

These skillsets may strike some board leaders as rather foreign to their responsibilities, but they are closely related to current thinking about good governance. For example, Chait, Ryan, and Taylor (2005, p. 79) have described "generative thinking" as an essential element of strong boards. Generative thinking is a cognitive process that, when given official support and a structure in board deliberations (which is the chair's role), can support good governance. It offers a think-tank mentality for moving a board forward through any kind of planning.

In many of the cases we studied, we see boards (whether consciously following Chait et al.'s framework or finding their way on their own) following generative thinking processes, including extrapolating meaning from their current processes, applying multiple organizational frames of reference (such as organizational policies and procedures, human resources, power and politics, and organizational culture), and using the past to frame the future (Chait, Ryan, and Taylor 2005).

Board chairs who led successful governance change in the associations we studied embraced the change process, educated themselves *with* or *in advance of* the board about group dynamics, got coached or coached others in effective group facilitation, and served as role models and early adapters. Mike Myatt (2012), a *Forbes* commentator, puts it bluntly:

> If you're not willing to embrace change you're not ready to lead. . . . Leadership is not a static endeavor. [It] demands fluidity . . . the willingness to recognize the need for change, and . . . the ability to lead change.

Summary

Board chairs can easily overlook their responsibility to not only manage the board's time effectively but also facilitate generative thinking on the part of all board members. Our cases describe many instances of board chairs and CEOs discovering together, through workshops or consultants, that they need to lead the board in a new way. The case of the American Camp Association that follows offers a particularly useful example of that principle.

A Call to Action and a Good Partnership Lead to Governance Change

Case: The American Camp Association

This is a story of a board investing in diversity to stay relevant. The "call to action" came from the CEO, but it took steady leadership from the chair to make it happen. This case is a bit longer than some, but that's because both partners in the governance change have plenty of good advice for association boards.

(continued)

(*continued*)

The American Camp Association (ACA) is a community of camp professionals who, for more than 100 years, have joined together to ensure the quality of camp programs. Organized in the state of Indiana, ACA is a 501(c)3 organization that collectively has an impact on 6.9 million campers and learners annually. Through the strategic planning process described further in this case, the association adopted three goals:

- Greater public understanding of and support for the value of the camp experience
- An increasing number of children, youth, and adults of all social, cultural, and economic groups with a camp experience
- Camp experiences of high quality

ACA's services to camping professionals include educational resources; research; policy work; outreach to parents, families, and other professionals to build safer, healthier, more fun environments where children and youth can become leaders; environmental stewardship; and promotion of public health. Their slogan: "Camp gives kids a world of good" (www.acacamps.org/about/who-we-are).

> *We had been through a name change and a rebranding. We did everything on the surface to look different but inside we weren't different.*

Challenge: A Name Change Doesn't Mean the Board Is Any Better

Peg Smith, CEO of ACA, described where the governance change began:

We had been through a name change and a rebranding. We did everything on the surface to look different but inside we weren't different.

Ann Sheets, currently the senior vice president of administration and finance for Camp Fire First Texas, and then president of the American Camp Association, recalls:

Peg was an association professional. A lot of what we did came as a result of some forward-thinking by Peg and looking at the association not from the "camp professional lens" but from a new perspective. When she was hired, we were going through a process of looking at the core services we were providing to our members. We had done a market study. We then changed our name. But we realized we had some fundamental problems. Our board did not include the kinds of people we needed in order to have the voice we wanted in the world.

Smith recalls the moment she delivered the news:

I believed that I had engendered a level of authenticity with the board and within the membership. But when I first presented the "call to action" to the board, it became eerily quiet. I was very worried—I wondered if I had blown all my social capital in one fell swoop. Then the conversation started.

Strategy: Board Chair Leads Conversation

Smith noted the important role that the board chair took in leading this conversation: "It was Ann's courage that challenged the board forward to 'do something different.'"

(*continued*)

(*continued*)

Sheets continued:

Sometimes if you stay around an organization long enough and participate in enough difficult discussions over the years, you will have some credibility. I was very fortunate to have previously been in a couple of leadership roles that allowed me to do this.

Smith described the difficult conversations that followed within the board:

Privately, there were many conversations that were very personal and often emotional. None of the books prepare you for the need for psychological hardiness. No one talks about what you have to be steeled for. There are moments when you really doubt what you have started. Change frightens people and people hate ambiguity.

Strategy: Leadership Commits to the Process

According to Smith, it was the board chair who provided the right amount of reassurance:

If not for Ann's leadership, the volunteer board members would not have been able to get through the messiness. When you have leadership that publically appears resolute and committed to a vision, that's inspiring and it allows change to unfold. Ann was always inspirational and enthusiastic about what the changes would ultimately mean. The initial commitment and willingness to embrace chaos happened under Ann's leadership. When it got tough and people wanted to quit trying, we both would say, "If not now, when?" The problems weren't going to go away.

We got that it was a complete package—governance, how we did business, everything. But we knew the first thing we had to do was change our governance.

Challenge: Loose Confederation Results in Anemic Performance

Smith recalled:

Previously we had about 26 independent moving parts (sections), a hybrid between franchises and a federation, each with its own board and staff. We all had the same intent, we were all using the same name and core services, but each had somewhat differing visions, missions, policies, and operations. We hung together very loosely and we weren't making an impact. The efficacy was anemic and this always kept us at a mediocre level of performance. Being a member in one part of the country didn't mean being a member in another part of the country— there were differences because of size, budget, geographic location, and so forth.

From the board seat, Sheets recalled: "With Peg's 'call to action' we realized we were simply not the association we wanted to be."

Challenge: Board Elections Are a Popularity Contest

Smith described a key problem for the board was coming to terms with its own selection process:

The national board was elected by popular vote with only about 10 percent of our membership voting. For the most part, it was

(continued)

(*continued*)

about those who were involved on a local level, who attended national conference, their name would become known, and then because they had a bit of national recognition, they were nominated. For some it was the culmination of their career.

We began to understand that if we really wanted the organization to make the difference we believed it could, the people sitting around the table today were probably not the people we needed to lead us. We had a very critical and brutal conversation about what needed to happen, with many sleepless nights and lots of uneasy conversations.

Strategy: Old Board Makes Way for New Board

Smith continued:

And then, at the end of the day, that board voted themselves out of office. From there we put a plan in place to transform the board and the entire association. Today, this is the most remarkable board I have worked with in 40 years. They are absolutely astounding. Some of this was serendipity, meaning the right people sitting there at the right time, but the rest is a credit to Ann's leadership.

Sheets recalled:

When we started, I don't think any of us realized how involved it would end up being. We were messing with norms, structures, and rituals that made up our culture—taking a hundred-year-old organization and trying to make it contemporary and relevant in our world today.

Strategy: Keep Focused on the Vision

Sheets also recalled:

> People get caught up in the bureaucracy of stuff. We continuously brought people back to the vision, the moral obligation. We got people out of the weeds, out of personality and politics. We kept the vision as our centerpiece and constantly referred back to it. It became a matter of people accepting what we called the Brutal Truths (for example, "It's not about camp; it's about making people better").

Strategy: Make Good Use of the Good Governance Tools

Smith described some of the tools ACA used:

> We applied Jim Collins's *Good to Great* and *Good to Great and the Social Sectors: Why Business Thinking Is Not the Answer*. Were the right people on our bus? You have to have a little of all of this: fear, brilliance, mistake, and luck. But again, the right leadership, the right timing in the history of the organization, the right background, and the right amount of education can make things happen. It was an amazing privilege to watch this creation.

Strategy: Come to Terms with Representational Governance

Sheets described a sequential combination of "understandings and strategies" that followed:

(continued)

(continued)

1. Governance cannot be representational and must be broader based. As a result the board canceled the next election.
2. Representation on the board should include half camp professionals and half professionals from other backgrounds (finance, marketing, youth development, education, psychology, etc.). It is no longer a popularity contest—it's now about what we need.
3. We needed greater diversity to mirror our constituents and society (race, age, sexual orientation). We were aging out and whiting out. We had a moral obligation to change because kids needed the experiences we provided. So we had to live through the uncomfortableness with having a different kind of board.

Strategy: Make Use of Task Forces

ACA established a 20/20 Task Force that started as a review of governance processes but then this went association-wide. Their ultimate recommendation was that every single element of the association had to recalibrate. For example, with 26 independent sections, each with its own board, the Task Force found that the national association had no control over the sections. So the goal became to have one association, not 26. This took a lot of conversation.

Strategy: Integrate the Plan, but Break It into Manageable Parts

With some internal statements and communication pieces (a "20/20 Statement" and a "20/20 Puzzle") the national board began to demonstrate to sections the case for integration. The heart of the process was a vision statement. The board used the process to demonstrate to change recipients that while the change was monumental, it could be broken into achievable stages. Thus ACA simplified a huge undertaking and reassured stakeholders.

Sheets explained:

We tried to give people a few things they could hang onto. We also had a roadmap: the logical steps we would have to take. It was ambiguous and people needed to see that, yes, there is a sequence and progress can be made little by little. We had to define that end vision. We also depended on our accountants and our lawyers— we needed the expertise that we were doing things that were right and would work and we were never outside the boundaries. They were available to us throughout the entire process.

Strategy: Exchange Leadership Roles When Necessary

Smith described the partnership ACA created to lead the change process:

Our attorney was as much a partner in this as Ann and I were—a triad. Also, Ann and I had very different skillsets and competencies and we worked off of each other to do this. One person takes the lead and the other drops back. It was an exchange of leadership without any thought of ego or positioning. At times we put the attorney in the lead position. We were able to use the talent we had around us continually. Who was the best? It can't be led by just one person because then it's just personality driven.

(continued)

(*continued*)

Mobilization and unification around the new mission and vision were facilitated by the legal unification of the organization as one association with one governing board. Strong local volunteer groups focused on operational elements of the plan. ACA employed several external consultants in the planning of the diversity goals, organizational changes, and human resources needs. They watched what the Girl Scouts, the Red Cross, and others were doing and examined what was working and where they were making mistakes.

Strategy: Take It at the Right Speed for Members

Smith explained that most of the major changes were accomplished by 2010, but the process was deliberately slowed:

> There was much concern about how certain people would be affected. We had to make some concessions that we would not make dramatic changes in operations for an additional two years. The final transformation is happening now (although there is never a final transformation if you are a dynamic and evolving organization). You have to have the commitment to hang tough and stick with it. If you give up too soon, you leave the whole association vulnerable.

Smith explained how the changes reinvigorated the board nomination process:

> Previously we barely had enough people to put up for election. After we made this change through an e-mail campaign, we were having 50 or more resumes submitted for consideration for the board, including from people we had never heard from before. We have a deliberate process of interviewing and matching up the skills for what we need. Since now, half of our board come

from other professions, most of the "others" are actively recruited. The external board members we now have are recommending others. They love being on this board. They find it challenging and advantageous to their own thinking.

The nomination process also succeeded in diversifying the board. Today, as Sheets described:

The age range is different, much younger than before. We changed the color. We changed the orientation (not just camp people—education, business, marketing, etc.). This was very intentional. We couldn't just hope for diversity to happen. We are now out networking and actively looking for people to recruit.

In the transformation process, the key milestones have included:

- The national board voting itself out of office, resulting in a change in the bylaws and development process.
- The national board rescinding a policy manual made of 157 "corrective" operational policies, and developing a whole new set of policies to focus on governance. The new manual expresses only critical limitations on operations and leaves staff and volunteers to determine *how* to reach goals.
- The national board voting to legally unify the organization.
- The emergence of key board members who served as "champions," providing critical ambassadorship to the local sections and others when emotions were high and discord erupted.
- Critical stakeholders emerging and transforming their club-like representative body into a leadership body.

(*continued*)

(*continued*)

- Members of the governing boards of the sections stepping forward and leading the way to eliminate their governing boards and thereby initiating new ways of work and interaction with the vision and purpose of the association.

In 2011, the ACA won a national award for its board transformation, BoardSource's *Prudential Leadership Award for Outstanding Nonprofit Boards*. Today, the ACA board, which for more than 100 years had been made up of mainly camp professionals, has been significantly diversified. New perspectives, demographics, geography, expertise, affiliations, skills, and competencies are in the boardroom. The board is focused on governing and strategic learning. The partnership between staff and volunteers working on operational issues is based upon a distributed leadership environment that shares ACA's vision for the future.

Now ACA describes itself as an organization whose capacity and impact has grown exponentially as a result of the governance and operational transformations. They are now "a movement with passion and purpose" where its collective voices and vision can make a better tomorrow for others.

The board's mantra has become "continual evolution":

The board's mantra has become continual evolution: "When you stop evolving, you become extinct." When you stop evolving, you become extinct—and that is not in the board's plan for the preferred future.

Both Sheets and Smith observed that with a commitment to continual evolution comes a commitment to continue to manage the challenges of building a strong board. Sheets noted:

The tougher part of the process is that you have to have *ambiguity-able* people. Each of us will run into a situation at some point in time where you just can't find in a book. And every organization is unique. Having people who can tolerate ambiguity contributes to success: people who can handle winding the way through to find meaning. In chaos, commitment, control, and challenge become huge issues, so psychological hardiness is critical—being able to understand that the only control you have is over your own actions.

> *You have to have* ambiguity-able *people. Each of us will run into a point of time you just can't find in a book.*

Smith added:

There is always a danger with any board that things become so familiar and so much is "this is the way we do it" that they miss one opportunity after another. Boards who try to lead that way, well, their organizations will not be around in the future.

As final words of advice, Sheets cautioned: "Don't underestimate the time it takes. Things are not going to happen overnight." Smith added: "Keep asking, 'What is the right thing to do?' Do it all with a sense of humor, a level of humility, and humanity." Sheets concluded: "And don't step into it without a good partner."

8

Working with External Consultants

I believe the real difference between success and failure . . . can be very often traced to the question of how well the organization brings out the great energies and talents of its people.

> —Thomas J. Watson, Jr., founder of IBM,
> *A Business and Its Beliefs* (1963)

As the case of the Northern Virginia Association of REALTORS® in Chapter 6 described, it can be hard for a board to know where to start a change process. Not every association will require an entire team of specialists, but all associations ignore at their own peril the value of leveraging existing knowledge. External consultants provide expertise to governance changes that may not be available internally. Given the emotional nature of change and change management, consultants provide the view of an objective outsider with no vested interest in outcomes. They help boards sort through needs, provide them with a broader frame of reference, coach them through leading change, and add credibility to the process with stakeholders. They also can save a board time and energy, and reduce experimentation, by bringing a portfolio of tested tools and strategies.

Block's (2000) description of a consultant as "a person in a position to have some influence . . . but who has no direct power to make changes" has particularly ambiguous meaning when the consultant is also brought in as an interim leader. As our cases reflect, the termination of an ineffective CEO may be followed by the hire of an interim executive. Such personnel may be brought in for short or long time periods, to keep a hand on the tiller while either supporting or facilitating the board's hire of a new CEO.

Concepts and Application

Engaging Board Consultants

As boards restructure, consultants serve many legal, organizational, financial, and facilitative roles. Our cases also described the involvement of attorneys and accountants, to name a few. A consultant can be brought in for group facilitation, organizational assessment and analysis, or to help guide a nonprofit association to think though a particular issue or problem, draft bylaws, restructure budgets, guide the board, or implement the change.

But the consultants most instrumental to board change will be those who specialize in organizational and board development. The vast majority of governance consultants available to the nonprofit sector, especially those in high demand and who come with excellent references, are very well versed on governance best practices and experienced in assisting an organization with change. The American Dental Education Association, whose case follows this chapter, involved a consultant who supported the board in leadership building, strategic direction, and organizational restructuring. In addition, with the consultant's help, ADEA completely reenergized the board by introducing out-of-the-box thinking to their board retreats. As remembered by ADEA Consultant, Joshua Mintz:

> This all came from the conversation around a desire to reenergize and rejuvenate, to have the board embrace something bigger— the lessons of leadership elsewhere, the context of community, the values we care about—and use these to inspire and reengage us. Following one retreat where we learned about George Washington and the Jay Treaty, one board member later said, "Last night I was thinking, and aren't we doing the same thing that Washington did? Why isn't ADEA looking at working more in a global culture?"

Engaging Interim Management

A particular kind of consultant, an interim leader, can provide either startup or transitional leadership in the case of a sudden loss or a planned turnover. Interim leadership is opportunity for an association to adopt a proactive response to change. Using an interim can provide a trained executive to steer the ship, providing day-to-day management and oversight while acting as an objective liaison to the board as the governing body focuses on the organization's strategic issues and the search. An interim can provide board and other staff breathing room and a facilitated opportunity for timely reflection about the specific qualities, skills, and experience needed in their next leader.

In a scenario where a longstanding executive director resigns suddenly, the interim leader not only can provide a smooth and orderly transition but also can make substantive—and long-overdue— improvements to the functioning of the organization. The interim can produce an organizational assessment and address specific operational issues so that the new executive then can hit the ground running without having to do a fix. Or the interim may be brought in so that the board can give a longtime, valued executive a sabbatical to prevent burnout and allow the executive to recharge batteries.

Jeffrey R. Wilcox, CRFE, president and chief executive officer of the Third Sector Company, describes the practice of short-term nonprofit executive leadership as being "in the midst of a significant landscape change from its traditional beginnings."

Today the marketplace offers interim management through private practitioners, practitioner cooperatives, nonprofit management support organizations, single-focused proprietary organizations, and multifaceted private firms that include interim management as a component of a larger suite of services. Today, the faces of interim executive management for nonprofit organizations are known to have assumed at least seven distinct roles in providing specialized leadership continuity:

1. The executive transition interim
2. The leave-of-absence interim
3. The new executive position interim
4. The organizational dissolution interim
5. The merger-and-acquisition interim
6. The court-appointed interim
7. The chief operating interim

Source: Wilcox (2014).

Successful Engagement of a Consultant

In addition to conducting appropriate reference checks, any consulting contract should be vetted by an association's legal counsel. The Compassion Capital Fund National Resource Center (2014) offers, through a publicly funded portal, a useful 40-page guide for engaging a consultant. To hire a consultant for any purpose, this manual observes the importance of thinking through goals, scope of work and authority, and deliverables.

Signing a Contract with a Consultant
- Define the scope of consulting to be provided and outline the expected deliverables. If a final written report is expected, be sure this is included in the contract.
- Ensure what the fee will be for the services to be provided. Understand how the consultant arrives at their fee.

- In the case of billable hours, understand what a "billable hour" means in their language, what is that hourly rate, and after defining the scope of consulting/expected deliverables, ask for an estimate with a not-to-exceed number of billable hours.
- Determine how the services will be provided (onsite, virtual, a combination thereof).
- Ensure there is a written and signed contract prior to the commencement of any services.
- Ensure that the contract has a termination clause.
- Ensure that the contract has a start date and end date, with a clause for extension if mutually agreed to in writing.
- If out-of-pocket expenses are to be incurred and reimbursed from the organization to the consultant, ensure that these are clearly spelled out in the contract and require receipts for payment.
- Ensure that there is a confidentiality clause.
- Ensure that there is a clause stating that the consultant is operating as an independent contractor and has no rights as an employee.
- Ensure that the contract contains any references to consultant insurance or bonding if appropriate.
- Ensure there is an indemnity clause.
- Require a W9 from the consultant upon contract signing.

Summary

In no instance in our interviews did we hear association leaders who regretted bringing in an organizational development and change consultant. They were more likely to tell us they wished they had done it sooner. Consultants—especially those who specialize in change management—bring a particularly valuable frame of reference. While they should be carefully vetted and supervised, clearly their involvement in nonprofit management and the enormous growth in the nonprofit consulting industry offers something of real value to governance change. The case of the American Dental Education Association that follows illustrates in greater detail how a good consultant can support successful governance change.

Using a Consultant to Improve the Leadership Lens of Governance

Case: American Dental Education Association

 Next time you take your child (or yourself) to the dentist, give a nod of thanks to the American Dental Education Association. ADEA's relevancy to dental education has never been stronger. Learn how a transformed board made it happen.

Founded in 1923, ADEA calls itself "The Voice of Dental Education," representing all U.S. and Canadian dental schools and many allied and advanced dental education programs, corporations, administrators, faculty, and students. Its mission is to lead institutions and individuals in the dental education community to address contemporary issues influencing education, research, and the delivery of oral health care for the overall health of the public (www.adea.org/about_adea/who_we_are/Pages/default.aspx).

Dr. Richard Valachovic came on as executive director of what was then known as the American Association of Dental Schools in 1997. At that time the association had an executive committee, which served as a governing board with 11 members, and a house of delegates, which served as its legislative body. Each year the house of delegates elected a president-elect, who subsequently moved into the president role and then became immediate past president. Seven member councils represented key constituencies like faculty, hospitals, and sections. Under the bylaws, the executive director was a voting member of the executive committee.

Challenge: Are We Still Relevant?

Valachovic described how the change process began:

Universities had closed seven dental schools in the 1980s and 1990s. Additional schools were in jeopardy of closing. A collective sensibility of the deans of key dental schools was that "we really need to do something. If these closures continue we're going to be in for some serious problems."

There was a lot of concern that we needed to demonstrate the value of dental education that dental schools, residency programs, and allied dental programs needed to show the public why oral health care was a critical part of overall health care. The National Institutes of Health reports that dental disease is a number one health priority.

We recognized that we needed to think differently about our mission and membership—that we needed to truly represent the entire dental education community, not only the dental schools. We formed a restructuring committee in 1998 that recommended expanding our membership to include allied dental education programs, advanced (specialty) programs, students, and corporate members. And we needed to model this expanded mission through our name, our brand and our governance. We needed to show that we were more than what we had been.

Valachovic cited a critical catalyst for change that was circulated to the leadership at the time, a report called "Dental Education at the Crossroads: Challenges and Change" (Institute of Medicine, Washington, DC, National Academy Press, 1995). The report observed that oral health care was not uniformly attainable across the nation and also noted the array of groups committed to improving access. The report highlighted common goals and opportunities for collaboration and innovation and galvanized the organization to look at everything differently. The House of Delegates took up recommendations in 2000.

(continued)

(*continued*)

Strategy: Restructure to Allow for Growth

Valachovic described the tasks:

> We went through a restructuring process because the old name, governance structure, and membership composition was not reflective of the mission and constituency we needed to represent in order to have impact. We needed to bring everyone under the umbrella. First, we changed our organization to the American Dental Education Association to reflect the fact that we were now representing every part of dental education.

Strategy: Create a More Inclusive Board Leadership Structure

> Then we changed our executive committee, which had really only been functioning as a committee that would manage the work of the association between the once-a-year delegate meetings. We needed to form a new board of directors that would no longer be perceived as a small, closed group of people. Moving to a board with representation from many stakeholder groups created more meaningful ways to foster engagement and inclusiveness throughout the association and lent credibility to the fact that we were representing everyone in dental education.

The entire restructuring process took place over two years. Dr. Lily T. Garcia, current board chair, offered this perspective:

> ADEA's board wasn't changing *because* of exponential growth but to *allow for* exponential growth, even more strategic changes in the organization. I became a member in 1994 and didn't join the board until 2008. In the beginning, from the outside, it

looked like there were just a few people managing everything. From this ground-level, new-member perspective, it didn't feel very inclusive. But things were changing.

Today, the whole role of the board has evolved. Decision making is not emotional or adversarial; it's healthy—they all offer their individual perspectives about their own constituencies, but all respond to the impact it would have on our association as a whole and for the good of all.

ADEA brought in Josh Mintz of the management consulting firm Cavanaugh, Hagan, Pierson & Mintz in 2002 to help ADEA with the changes, including leadership building and organizational restructuring. Mintz recalled the importance of creating clear expectations about service on the ADEA board:

The new board composition represents the entire spectrum of the membership. When the board comes together, the different perspectives brought by the seven councils add great value, but it's also a challenge for board members to balance "representing their constituency" and thinking about the greater good for the association as a whole. There's a lot of commonality in goals, but we still have multimillion dollar enterprises sitting next to individual faculty members. Their perspectives and interests can be really different.

This makes the conversation pretty rich. The fiduciary part is easy. On the policy part, the right balance takes some learning. In the first year, you often see a new board member say, "On behalf of our constituency . . ." but quickly learn not to look at decision making solely in that way. They adopt the appropriate fiduciary duty of loyalty. It's part of the culture. But there is definitely a learning curve and some give-and-take on the part of the whole board. Where appropriate, the individual constituency voice is being listened to and is part of the process.

(continued)

(*continued*)

Another big area of change was the way the board conducted its meetings. Valachovic explained:

What we learned from the initial experience of school closures is that our board must be proactive. We need to always have a good evidence base to respond to issues. So we begin every board meeting with a discussion of the changing environment for our work.

For example, even before the Affordable Care Act became law, we were discussing its impact on dentistry. We had to know what an "essential dental benefit" meant. If we were going to increase the number of children coming into dental offices, what did that mean for dental education and how we prepare the future workforce? If it was going to increase the number of Medicaid patients, what did that mean for dental education?

We were successful at building coalitions to advocate for including pediatric dental care as an essential benefit in the ACA. So today, every kid in the country now has access to oral healthcare because of that work.

Board chair Garcia noted that ADEA has a policy center to give the board the data and information needed for meaningful discussions. The outcome, according to Valachovic, is:

Our board now comes to the table with a pretty good handle on what the issues are and they don't get bogged down in the weeds or involved in operations such as how a policy is carried for by the staff after a decision is made. We come with a common language and evidence for our conversations and from there comes decision making. Our meetings are run that way by our chairs and this has really worked out very well.

Mintz observed:

Many associations start a board meeting "getting the basics out of the way first," leaving the discussions of key strategic issues until later in the agenda. Inevitably, the meeting runs long, and the substantive strategic discussion either gets abbreviated or deferred to the next meeting. At ADEA, the board meeting begins in the afternoon and the first item for discussion is a "mega-issue" conversation. This is followed by dinner together that first night where the conversation typically continues in a less formal environment. The more typical fiduciary grunt-work of the board is pushed off to the second day of the meeting.

ADEA also uses its annual board retreats as a means to shift board culture and encourage big strategic thinking. A new design to the retreats increased the board's capacity to make big, bold conceptual leaps in their deliberations.

Previously the board retreats were essentially extended board meetings with the same format and people, just more time. Valachovic thought, "Let's find something new." So he asked Josh Mintz, the consultant, to help him design a more engaging day of learning. It was to be outside of their "dental box," so to speak. Valachovic wanted to take his board somewhere to learn about leadership and then apply those lessons to the association.

Over the years, the board has been to Mount Vernon to study the leadership lessons of George Washington, to the Folger Shakespeare Library to learn about the politics of leadership using Julius Caesar, and to the National Museum of the American Indian to explore non-Western models of leadership. They visited New Orleans to learn about leadership in the response to Hurricane Katrina. And this past year, they met with Robert Parris Moses, leader of the Mississippi Freedom Project on leadership in the civil rights era.

(continued)

(continued)

Valachovic explained the impact on the board:

Going somewhere on a learning journey together not only builds board relationships, which is hugely important, but provides an opportunity to look at different models of leadership. This took a huge leap of faith on the part of our board members. We were asking them to take time to learn about something completely unrelated to dental education and then apply those lessons to our field. But it has been hugely successful and resulted in a totally different way in which our board now talks about things.

Garcia was enthusiastic:

I love it. Each year, the chair has the opportunity to identify a theme that is meaningful to them and to help design a learning event that builds off of that topic. For me, that was the civil rights era. It is not necessarily about dental education. It's about what makes us leaders.

Concluded Garcia:

I don't know how one can explain the unintended consequence of positive change—how this change in culture affects our feelings about ADEA—unless you have been actively engaged in the change. What you went into and what you are now a part of are two different organizations. We went from good to great and still have more and even greater possibilities ahead and you think, this is bigger than you. It's inspiring. And it's fun.

9 | Getting the Most from Assessment and Evaluation

True genius resides in the capacity for evaluation of uncertain, hazardous, and conflicting information.

—Winston Churchill

Executive Director Jim Miller of the League of Minnesota Cities explained how in the process of board change, the organization relied on regular informal and scheduled formal assessment and evaluation:

We used to do conventional strategic planning at each September's board retreat. This has now evolved from setting longer-term goals to reviewing annual items that are more urgent (e.g., how are our cities doing financially and how can we help them through their crises.) Our strength is that we can step back once a year and ask, "How are we doing, and is there a need for change?"

But a weakness we recognized was that we always came away with more things to do (objectives, tactics), but we were never taking anything off the table. So we are now experimenting with something we are calling "strategic review"—which has elements of a conventional strategic planning process but does not carry the expectation that anything new will come immediately from the exercise. We ask how we are doing as an organization. Then we do an environmental scan: What's on the horizon? What do we need to be aware of? Where might we spend more time on in the coming year? What are the questions we need to be addressing?

The League intersperses these activities with regular (every three years) "governance retreats" separate from the strategic review effort and governance assessments, using the BoardSource board self-assessment tool. These activities sometimes changed the board's priorities, as the case that follows this chapter reflects.

Assessment and evaluation of governance processes require two things: stated goals and a process for measuring the board's progress in reaching them. Since there is no single or generic model of governance, how boards actually fulfill their responsibilities will vary enormously. But recognizing that board performance, like organizational performance, varies over time also means that governance performance measures should not only fit each organization's circumstances but should also be renewed and refreshed periodically (Ingram 2003).

This chapter introduces three levels of assessment that support governance change and in which board members should be involved: organizational strategic assessments, board self-assessments, and process assessments designed for measuring the actual quality of the deliberations. From the macro- to micro-level, each has value to change management.

Concepts and Application

Organizational Strategic Assessment

Boards are advised to monitor and evaluate an organization's progress in fulfilling its mission and meeting previously established goals

(Butler 2007). Evaluation in the context of mission-fulfillment for a nonprofit helps to inform policymaking. Staff facilitate this process with accurate information, but the task is not accomplished simply by filling board members' mailboxes with excessive and overly detailed data.

Although there are many options, each with advantages and disadvantages, many of our interview subjects favored "dashboard reporting," which makes it possible to present succinct, easily readable performance indicators that allow the board to view organizational status at a glance. The effectiveness of these performance measurement formats in scholarly assessments is still being explored, but interest in their use has certainly increased (see, for example, Kaplan 2001). Proponents of dashboard reports describe them as early warning devices, similar to an automobile's lights and signals, to help leaders assess setbacks and to focus the board's attention on what matters most (Butler 2007). Without knowing whether the use of these tools is imitative or based on evidence of success, it was clear from our interviews that they helped board members not only assess an organization's strategic progress but also keep on task and focused on strategic issues.

Board Self-Assessment

In prior governance studies, researchers have found a strong connection between boards that self-assessed and better board performance (Board-Source 2013; Gazley and Bowers 2013; Harrison and Murray 2014). The causal path is not clear—do high-performing boards self-evaluate more as a best practice, or are these boards performing better because they have evaluated themselves and then fixed identified governance problems? Regardless of the implications, BoardSource observes on its website that "assessment is the most effective way to ensure your board members understand their duties and utilize effective good governance practices." Yet, data still suggest that approximately half of all boards do not monitor their own performance, and most of those who do still do not use a formal self-assessment instrument (Gazley and Bowers 2013; Ostrower 2007).

Nonetheless, a board self-assessment is an efficient way to get input from all board members and to compare performance against generally accepted standards, and it should be put to greater use. Assessment can also be used to build a shared understanding of the board's responsibilities (Harrison and Murray 2014). By determining what should be assessed, the board in effect is deciding what really matters. When a board engages in an assessment process, it is checking in on the board's perceptions, individually and collectively, of its own performance.

Responses to self-assessment tools should be carefully analyzed and discussed with the full board, as they offer an opportunity to discuss levels of board member participation and engagement. They can also assess the degree of consensus at which individual board members perceive various aspects of their own performance. It may be useful to explore responses with a low degree of consensus to understand the diversity of opinion among the board. Such an analysis also helps a board prepare for larger governance decisions. A periodic board member self-assessment that is not given much extra attention may serve as a starting point for a larger, generative discussion about the board's collective capacity to make decisions and lead a governance change.

Meeting Evaluations and Other Process Evaluations

As the following case of the League of Minnesota Cities demonstrates, it's also valuable to consider using meeting evaluations to assess a board's readiness, progress, and ability to achieve change. Meeting evaluations are also used in assessments of the health of team dynamics (see Chapter 5). Meetings, after all, are the structure in which governance occurs: good meeting, good outcomes; bad meeting, often bad outcomes.

Each board member's perception of and experience in a meeting is individual. Allowing an opportunity to regularly provide feedback about what works well and what doesn't can lead to important process improvements such as the length of the agenda, the quality of the discussion, or the opportunity for participation. The meeting assessment, even in organizations that feel they already have strong cultures of participation, also signals that leaders respect each board member's time and commitment.

Our interviews demonstrated that a successful meeting evaluation can be a five-minute around-the-table discussion at the end of each meeting: "How do you feel this meeting went? Were we successful? Did we achieve what we set out to do in our agenda?" Or, board members can complete a written evaluation form. Follow-up is important to address any areas at issue. A sample meeting evaluation form is included in the Tools section in the appendix of this book.

Summary

There's little reason to cover detailed ground when it comes to organizational performance assessment. Plenty of resources are available for association boards generally. What may be less self-evident is how they have been effectively used in change management processes, hence the value of this research (Harrison and Murray 2014). The three strategies introduced here will help associations understand that boards have multiple process evaluation tools at their disposal, each capable of assessing the organization at different levels, as an organization, a governing board, or a single event. The case that follows introduces several means of gathering information and assessing progress, including a tool that may be less familiar to boards: an exit interview for outgoing board members.

Formal and Informal Assessment Supports Governance Change

Case: League of Minnesota Cities

 This local government-serving association had no competitors and no membership retention challenges, but a personnel and leadership crisis still resulted due to board inattention. Learn how a staff-driven board reinvented itself into a collaborative, accountable governing body, relying on a long list of board development and assessment activities.

The League of Minnesota Cities was founded in 1913 by a special law passed by the Minnesota Legislature. Initially part of the Extension Division of the University of Minnesota, the League became independent in 1974. Today, the League's membership includes 800 member cities and their elected and appointed officials, as well as a number of special municipal districts and townships. Its mission is to promote excellence in local government through effective advocacy, expert analysis, and trusted guidance for all Minnesota cities, including education and training, policy development, risk management, and other services.

Following a common model across the U.S. states, membership is voluntary yet the League enjoys virtually 100 percent of the potential membership population in the state. Membership retention has never been a problem, a point about which Executive Director Jim Miller is rightly proud:

> We are a multiservice, soup-to-nuts kind of organization. We represent cities at the legislature, provide training, conduct research, and provide inquiry assistance for our members. We have a department of six or seven attorneys who do nothing but respond to approximately 4,000 inquiries from our members each year. We assist members with human resource management questions. We are the major insurance provider for most

Minnesota cities. We provide an investment program for our member cities.

Challenge: Board Realizes It Has Been Remiss

Before Jim Miller arrived, the organization was functioning well in many respects. But it had recently gone through a sudden leadership change necessitated by several serious personnel problems and signs of growing member dissatisfaction. Most of the board members felt surprised by the problems, but they also realized they had been remiss in fulfilling their duties. This was the catalyst that framed Miller's early years. And one of his first challenges was to restore confidence.

Executive director since 1993, Miller was just coming from a board meeting on the afternoon we interviewed him, so governance was very much on his mind:

Before I arrived the board was more reactive than participatory. Staff led the organization. The board was not strategic or generative, although they were undertaking their fiduciary responsibilities well.

So, when several employees brought problems to the attention of a few board members, the entire board moved quickly to address them.

Joining Miller in the interview, current board president David Osberg described how the problems felt to the League's municipal members:

I began serving in a town in 1992. Early in my career, I was not actively involved in the League. The problems were kept at board level, internal. For the most part, the membership was never aware. In retrospect, you realize how good it is now and

(continued)

(*continued*)

> how bad it was then. You don't know what you are missing until you get something better.

Challenge: Monopoly Market Results in Benign Neglect

Miller acknowledged the League's monopolistic market position was also a challenge for the League, since it failed to motivate the board. He felt that members deserved more, and it didn't take long for the League board to recognize this point and adopt some good governance practices, first by strengthening the board–staff partnership:

> It was pretty clear (but not really intentional), that back then the board operated in the mode of benign neglect. No one really thought about the respective roles of the board and management. And there was no attention to building the competencies of the board.

Strategy: Build Open Board–Staff Dialogue

> Today there is a culture between board and staff that I would characterize as one of comfortable collaboration. Over time our board has developed a great deal of trust in the staff, and conversely the staff values the board's input into our work. It really is a partnership. It's not about protecting roles. We're very open about bringing items to the board and asking for their input. And the board has a very comfortable relationship with the staff. They feel free to talk to the right staff people to get information if they need it. And the staff understands the board's ultimate fiduciary responsibility. They have the kind of relationship that only comes from a high level of trust that has developed over the years.

From the board seat, Osberg observed:

What I really appreciate about Jim's leadership is how he presents information, for example, the budget. He walks the board through it and even though he and the staff have first-hand information and have worked diligently to create the budget, he says, "You [the board] have the right to shape it as you see fit—this is just our recommendation."

Strategy: Use Task Forces and Working Groups to Keep Thoughts Broad and Generative

Miller noted:

We've relied fairly frequently on putting together working groups and task forces with joint board and staff participation to broaden the thinking on the issues we are working through. It's a symbiotic relationship. I've come to understand that it doesn't happen accidently. It takes a board that places a premium on their responsibilities and a staff that keeps the important issues in front of them.

Strategy: Ensure Prospective Board Members Are Ready to Govern

The League's nominations process begins with an open call for those interested in serving on the nominating committee. The president appoints the members from board members and the general membership. Their charge is to interview prospective board members and recommend a slate for election by the general membership. When someone decides to apply, they get a copy of the League's Governance Handbook.

(continued)

(continued)

Miller explained:

> During the interview process we make sure that they answer and ask questions about our expectations, how we want individuals to act as a board member. We ask: "Did you read the governance handbook? Do you agree with it? Is there anything in there you would have trouble following?" We take this seriously.

New board members then attend a half-day orientation to acquaint them with the operations of the League, staff responsibilities, and the mission. This orientation not only introduces board members to a complex organization, with 102 full-time employees, 55 contract employees, and five different legal entities, it cements expectations about staff roles versus board roles.

Strategy: Evaluate Board Meetings

The board meets a minimum of 10 times a year, for about three hours each meeting. Every meeting concludes with an evaluation, which a governance committee reviews quarterly. Osberg explained how the evaluations are used:

> We have a pretty high return from our board members on the meeting evaluations. And we try to be cognizant of the responsibility for a board member to read packets in advance of the meeting (the duty of care). I work to encourage our board members to understand and adhere to this important responsibility. Jim does a good job of structuring the agenda so we know what actions need to be taken. The routine, pro forma reporting is placed in a consent agenda, so we've gotten pretty good over the years at focusing on the things that we need to pay attention to: "Here is the material piece of this topic you want to give

consideration to. This is the crux of what the board ought to consider."

Miller noted:

We try to structure agenda items to frame issues with viable solutions or alternatives where possible. If it is a topic that has possible alternatives, we outline the strengths and weaknesses of each.

Strategy: Invest in "Generative" Discussions

The League's board has also brought in Bruce Lesley from BoardSource to facilitate retreats. The board currently is discussing *Governance as Leadership* (Chait, Ryan, and Taylor 2005), including opportunities to structure discussions into "fiduciary," "strategic," or "generative," modes. Miller explained how that strategy changed the way the board operates:

We used to do conventional strategic planning at each September's board retreat. This has evolved from looking at longer term goals to reviewing annual items that are more time sensitive (e.g., How are our cities doing financially and how can we help them through their crises?). Our strength is that we can step back once a year and ask, "Where are we going, how are we doing?"

Strategy: Reassess Priorities and Capacity

But a weakness we recognized was that we always came away with more things to do (objectives, tactics) even though we were never taking anything off the table. So we are now

(continued)

(*continued*)
    experimenting with something we are calling "strategic review"
    [addressed in more detail at beginning of chapter].

These environmental scans, governance retreats, and assessments have sometimes changed the board's priorities. Osberg recalled:

I remember when the 2007 financial crisis hit and cities were severely distressed. Jim and the board threw out any idea of doing strategic planning. It was more like "all hands on deck." Jim understood that cities in financial crisis would need to rely on us more. It was tactical not to add any more to our plate. It was about keeping our collective heads above water.

Strategy: Flexible Knowledge Management Tools

Miller also discussed the value of regular, open communication with the board, and recommended that association boards not rely overly on formal CEO reports. Instead, he suggested:

In between board meetings, I do a written interim report related to follow-up on actions that the board has taken at previous meetings or something that will never make it to the board level but that may be of interest or necessary for them to know. This has become a pretty important piece to add continuity between meetings, keeping board members attached to the organization. And this allows us to be more efficient in the use of board time when they do meet.

    We also regularly encountered new board members asking "newbie" questions about history and past documents. This led us a conversation about how we can make sure that board members have access to all the information they need. We created a Sharepoint site (a form of knowledge management) with all of our past board and organizational materials. This board portal has paid numerous dividends to our work.

Challenge: Board Turnover Means Expertise Is Lost

The League, like many of our interview subjects, also faced the challenge of building board expertise when term limits require board member turnover. The League's solution to the problem was to conduct formal exit interviews (see ahead) with outgoing board members and to get new board members up to speed faster. As Miller explained:

Turnover brings in new blood, but having to get new blood up to speed so we don't lose momentum is hard. So we are always working on developing the board relationships.

Strategy: Mentoring for the Incoming and Exit Interviews for the Outgoing

We often heard from our departing board members as they left their seat, "You know, the first year I wasn't quite as comfortable as I wanted to be, the second year I was coming around, and the third year I felt like I was making major contributions, and then I'm off." We began to realize that we needed to increase our board member capacity to contribute sooner. Right after being elected, each new board member is appointed a board-member mentor (a second- or third-year member). The mentor calls the board member before each meeting, sits with the new board member, and answers any specific questions a new board member has. We have found this to be a very effective practice.

David Osberg observed:

A wonderful result of the mentor program is the depth of a friendship that develops that might have not existed if not for the mentor program.

(continued)

(continued)

The League has also worked on board-level and board–staff team building. They brought in a facilitator to conduct a Parker Team Player Survey (a personality assessment tool) with a structured discussion on how each board member approaches his or her job, and how each board member's strengths can be assets to the board team. Miller recalled:

> I was very surprised how much the board enjoyed that activity; they have now said they want to do this every year.

Strategy: Don't Get Complacent All Over Again

These activities, and the financial stability they have supported, have allowed the League to focus much more on future planning and visioning. While Jim Miller was pleased with the League's status, he observed the risks of complacency:

> In today's board meeting, one board member pointed out 50 percent of our revenue comes from one source. She asked, "Is that a threat?" I said, "Yes, theoretically, but probably not likely." But that comment has now got us thinking that we need to keep an eye on this.
>
> Thinking that the way that we are providing member services today will continue to be the way we will be providing them in the future is not realistic. How do we really utilize technology that provides convenience and maximizes services to our membership? We have to continue to look at this.
>
> Another issue is, how do we attract the new generations? How do we really get them involved? Within the organization we are doing succession planning because lots of people are nearing retirement. The board has spent a lot of time working on

a succession plan for my position and now has in place the process they will follow when the time comes to replace me.

Board Member Exit Interview

Questions

- How could you have been better prepared to start your board term?
- How would you describe your overall board experience? Did you feel your talents and experience were used and your perspective respected? Do you feel you were able to make a contribution?
- What were the biggest challenges to you in performing your board responsibilities?
- What could the board or staff have done to improve your experience?
- Did you feel the expectations of you as a board member were realistic? If not, why not?
- How do you think the board as a whole functions? What improvements to meetings or structure would you suggest?
- Knowing what you do now, would you recommend board service to others?

Source: League of Minnesota Cities.

Conclusion
Strategies and Resources for Success

We are the ones we've been waiting for.
                    —Alice Walker, author and activist

In our interview, Marty Saggese, executive director of the Society for Neuroscience, offered the *Tao Te Ching* quote: "In the universe great accomplishments are made up of small deeds." When he arrived at the society, board members were not happy with their recent governance experience but were unsure about what changes were needed. He understood that the board had not felt well-served toward the end of his predecessor's tenure. The association required a different model of staff interaction with the board.

His deputy executive director, operations, Kate Hawker, concurred. She described the origin of the big procedural changes that followed as a very subtle and intentional cultural shift that happened around the time Saggese arrived. And change was built brick by brick through communication, training, and focus. Today they have great

213

board–staff relationships—a respect that has been hard-earned on both sides through intentional efforts.

Change is evidenced by end results of some kind. But it is the journey, the day-to-day commitment to moving forward with vision and intention, those "small deeds"—that bring about these results.

For those prepared to take this journey, it is hard to cleanly summarize the recommendations of such a diverse group, some of whom arrived at better governance using strategies entirely at odds with those recommended by others, and some of whom executed similar change strategies but in quite a different order. Some associations, for example, began the change process with a bylaws revision. Others ended there. Some considered a more risk-averse board to be a good outcome for their change process, while others praised their improved boards for being bigger risk-takers.

But there are clear patterns in our findings. First are the collective goals. These are boards that sought governance change to become more strategic, representative, nimble, and knowledgeable—all aimed at serving their members better. Next are patterns in their strategies. Many in our study found the following were necessary to achieve the kind of smart, resilient, flexible, strategic, and entrepreneurial board of directors we have been writing about:

- Shorter bylaws, to give the board flexibility
- More nimble (e.g., shorter) strategic planning documents.
- A smaller board (while a few associations increased their board size to gain more capacity, most shrank the size of their board)
- Fewer standing committees and greater use of task forces and working groups, again with the goal of flexibility via ad-hoc assignments
- More frequent board meetings, to maintain the pace of change and the focus on strategic thinking
- Consent agendas, to free up the board's time for generative discussion
- More carefully structured meetings, to keep board members on task

- More skill-based board recruitment, to ensure members bring *more* than representative value
- Active if not constant efforts at identifying and preparing new board leaders
- Carefully managed board member selection, to ensure representative goals can be achieved with a smaller board size
- Frequent if not constant self-education in board governance, to ensure members understand stakeholder and regulatory expectations
- Evaluation of themselves as individuals and also of their board's governance processes
- Patience and trust

In addition to these patterns in the elements of the change process that reflect the *how* of transformational governance, we also found patterns in the *what*—specifically, what needed to change in order to achieve these goals. Among our 50-plus fully interviewed associations, nearly all (more than 90 percent) described changes to at least one of the following governance elements:

- Bylaws (e.g., to shorten them and facilitate quicker board action)
- Policies and procedures (to accommodate the shorter bylaws)
- Board roles and responsibilities (mostly to focus the work of the board on strategic rather than operational activities)
- The structure of board meetings (e.g., to free up board time for more strategic activities or to improve the board's culture)
- The structure of committees and committee roles (to increase flexibility or to delegate more board tasks to the committee level)
- Board member eligibility (mainly to reduce reliance on constituency-based boards and achieve new knowledge, skills, or representation)

Thus, these patterns suggest that while in many examples the structures and functions of governance shrank, the boards in these associations ended up spending *more* time governing, just in less rule-bound and more nimble and efficient governance systems. Boards that invested in these changes in turn generated new benefits for themselves, including more efficient and effective decision making, greater collegiality, and a stronger focus brought about by the alignment of mission, culture, and strategy. We heard many stories of positive secondary effects, such as the ability to hire better staff who would be reluctant to work with a weak board. And in many instances, interviewees discovered that growth and improvement offered new challenges, but they also noted that their stronger expertise and board culture gave them better tools for dealing with challenges. Dorsey, of Professional Ski Instructors of America (PSIA) and the American Association of Snowboard Instructors (AASI), observed:

> Another challenge is that we have been successful. Two outcomes for us: First is that the board can sometimes be complacent. Our solution has been to feed them outside literature so that they understand the external environment. As a result we were one of the first associations to evolve to the new 990 form. Second, we now have record membership numbers and sponsorship revenue, and more technological sophistication that enabled this success.

But as the previous list of potentially necessary changes to governance processes reflects, nonprofits must anticipate a real commitment of time and energy to go down the same path. Among the 44 associations that provided us an estimate of the time required to complete a governance transformation, one third (32%) reported an investment of one to two years, 39 percent reported three to five years, and the remaining 30 percent reported the process took six or more years.

Summary

We conceived this study from the beginning as an exploration of a journey toward good governance. According to those organizations we studied, one of the healthier outcomes of that perspective may be that they find the work of good governance is never done. Rather, these organizations perceive themselves to be in a now-continual process of self-assessment and improvement. What sets these associations apart is a willingness to embrace the journey and not just the destination. The organizational leaders we interviewed loved to learn, and enjoyed the feeling of self-efficacy that came with facing new challenges with a much bigger skillset. The capacity for a board to learn was, perhaps, in the end the single most important quality of these boards in their journey to high performance. We end, therefore, on a similar note to where *What Makes High Performing Boards* left off, observing that "a high-functioning board may not have all of the answers, but it's willing to invest in learning them" (Gazley and Bowers 2013).

Thanks for taking the journey with us. It's time to roll up your sleeves and get to work.

Appendix
Tools and Resources

Tools

Team and Group Dynamics

Tuckman and Jensen (1977) used a rather limited research study to describe a five-part model of team building that—while not necessarily predictive or linear in all cases—has become enormously popular with both educators and practitioners. The stages of *forming*, *storming*, *norming*, *performing*, and *adjourning* capably describe the challenges that team members face as they learn to work together. Boards of directors, similarly, must learn the elements of good team dynamics. Although the Tuckman model is presented here in stage sequence, it is important to note that teams will work on all elements of all stages and

Source: B. W. Tuckman and M. A. Jensen, "Stages of Small Group Development Revisited," *Group and Organizational Studies* 2, no. 4 (1977): 419–427. Reprinted by permission of SAGE.

sequential movement may occur both in a forward (developmental) and backward (regressive) direction.

Forming

During the forming stage of a team, there is an orientation to the model being used, identification of customers, and analysis of customer needs. The team leader and team facilitator also work to resolve dependency issues through team building activities. The overall emphasis is one of awareness. The stage concludes when team members understand and are committed to the goal of continuous quality improvement (commitment) and relate to each other in a friendly, concerned, and professional manner (acceptance).

Storming

Conflict is the general theme of the storming stage. Defining and measuring a process to improve provides an early opportunity for different perspectives and alternatives to emerge. Task resistance and relationship hostility are common. These behaviors and attitudes will not always be loud and obvious; resistance and hostility may appear as silence, missed meetings, reduced focus, or stubbornness. The second stage ends when team members acknowledge and confront conflict openly (clarification) and listen with understanding to others (belonging).

Norming

By the beginning of the norming stage, the process for continuous improvement has been selected, stated in measurable terms, and measured prior to any attempt to improve it. The general theme of cooperation appears as open communication increases concerning the task and team relationships become more cohesive. Teams explore the process more thoroughly using a variety of quality tools (i.e., Pareto charts, fishbone diagrams, flowcharts, etc.) in order to gain a deeper understanding before developing solutions. Frequently teams will encounter additional conflicts during this stage and regress to storming behavior that must then be resolved for movement into the norming stage again. The norming stage concludes when team members include others in the decision-making process (involvement) and recognize and respect individual differences (support).

Performing

In the performing stage, the team works interdependently and engages in problem solving. The productivity theme involves the development of a solution and a plan of implementation that includes a measurement of progress toward the goal of improving a process. This stage ends when team members contribute ideas and solutions to the problem (achievement) and value the contributions and ideas of others (pride).

Adjourning

The final stage of adjourning brings the team to closure and results in a theme of separation. The team terminates the task of process improvement and disengages from the relationships formed during the life of the group. Celebration and summarization, as well as some publicity concerning task accomplishment, are common activities during this time. This stage concludes when team members recognize and reward team performance (recognition) and encourage and appreciate comments about team efforts (satisfaction).

Stages of Team Development

Stage	Potential Behaviors	Feelings	Potential Productivity
Forming	Attempts to define the task Attempts to determine team norms Focus on the "self" as opposed to the team Polite High-level discussions Team members testing the leader Complaints Discussions about why "it" won't work	Nervous Pride for being selected Excitement Optimism Fear Anxiety	Low
Storming	Arguing Differences of opinion Defensiveness Quietness Interruptions Team members not listening Round-and-round discussion	Resistance Fluctuations and shifts in attitude toward the team or task Frustration	Low
Norming	Attempts to reduce conflict More personal sharing and confiding in each other Team norms are respected A shift in the focus from the self to the team	A sense of team spirit camaraderie Acceptance as a team member Relief that work will get done	Medium
Performing	Individuals begin looking at their behaviors and self-adjusting	Satisfaction with work Energized Sense of belonging	High

Stages of Team Development (*continued*)			
Stage	**Potential Behaviors**	**Feelings**	**Potential Productivity**
	Team solves problems together Supportiveness and attachment within the team		
Adjourning	Closure Celebration	Sadness Pride of accomplishment	

Source: B. W. Tuckman and M. A. Jensen, "Stages of Small Group Development Revisited," *Group and Organizational Studies* 2, no. 4 (1977): 419–427. Reprinted by permission of SAGE.

Team Ground Rules

Ground rules are important because:

- Behaviors are a significant component that create team culture.
- Norms bring context in which to discuss productive and non-productive group behaviors.
- Common understanding and agreement up front of how the team will behave together can prevent misunderstandings, conflict, and disagreements.

Team Ground Rules Worksheet

Ground Rule	What does the behavior look like?	How will we ensure that it happens?

Source: Elise Yanker, Collaborative Consulting, Inc.

Sample Communications Guidelines

Purpose:
- Today's gathering is to help us explore and develop consensus about where we are and where we are going.
- We intend for this gathering to help strengthen relationships within the board team, reconfirm our commitment to NAME, and build our understanding of our governance.
- We will agree up front that we may not all always agree with everything by the end of today's process or beyond. But we also agree up front that our common desire, as members of a governance team and as volunteers who guide and provide support for NAME, that we will commit to finding a way for consensus to emerge and, that once consensus has been developed, such consensus will be supported by the entire board to each other, to _____, and to the public.
- We move anything that will require future discussion by the board to a "parking lot" and charge NAME's board president to follow up as needed and on a timely basis by placing these on future board meeting agendas.

Cell Phones:
- I will turn off my cell phone and agree not to use it during our gathering today.

Speaking:
- I will speak in the first person and from personal experience.
- I may share my first-person experience *only* at the appropriate time.
- I will take a moment of silence if I feel disturbed. This is to find my own inner peace.
- I will work to avoid judging or arguing.
- No Zingers. Zingers are sideways communications in an attempt to create humor that are statements that appear to be funny or friendly teasing, that are sarcastic, or that are self-deprecating. The conscious may see this just as humor but the subconscious sees this as an "ouch." This is because your subconscious cannot make the difference between fact and fantasy. When there is a Zinger, there is no

need for the group to discuss it. Someone should just say, "Zinger" and then everyone can clear the air by saying together, "Out of Here," by gesturing hands over the shoulders.

Listening:
- I listen actively to whomever is speaking, sending my respect and compassion. This includes a commitment that I will not interrupt other speakers, I will not conduct other tasks while listening, and I will work to ensure my understanding of what is being said. If needed, I will take notes to later ask clarifying questions.
- I allow one person to speak at a time, without interruption.
- I do not engage in side conversations or ask questions of any other group member when someone else is speaking.
- When I want to speak, I agree to raise my hand and wait to be acknowledged by the designated facilitator.
- I will not leave the room while someone else is making a point and will only leave the room if absolutely necessary. This is so that I can have the same understanding as the rest of the group by hearing and participating in all discussion.

Intention:
- I respect the confidentiality of what people may share and agree to honor it.
- I recognize that I am not here to learn how to exert my power and personal perspectives to change others. I am here to listen, try to understand other viewpoints, share my viewpoints, and work with this team to find the most positive and constructive path forward to develop consensus for governance, which is part of my fiduciary responsibility as a nonprofit board member.

When Guidelines Are Not Followed:
- There are times when the guidelines are not followed by the group. I am free to mention this to the group. I will raise my hand and say, "I am noticing that the communication guidelines are not being followed."

Source: Adapted from Gerald G. Jampolsky, PhD

Board Member Agreement

As a Board member serving on behalf of the NAME OF ORGANI-ZATION, my signature below indicates my highest commitment to our patients and community, a passion for the stated mission, the agreement to ensure that the business of NAME OF ORGANIZATION is conducted with the highest level of integrity, and my willingness to be an enthusiastic, involved, and positive Board team player.

As a reminder, by agreeing to serve on the board of a nonprofit organization, a board member owes a fiduciary duty to the nonprofit he or she is serving. Board members are required to take off their personal or "constituent member" hat and put on their "board member" hat. In performing his or her duties, a director must act in the best interests of the nonprofit organization for whom he or she is serving (i.e., work to fulfill the nonprofit's tax-exempt purposes and maintain its tax-exempt status).

In general, the duties that a director owes the nonprofit are:

Duty of Loyalty

As a Board member and representative of NAME OF ORGANIZA-TION, I understand that I am required to act *solely* in the best interests of NAME OF ORGANIZATION rather than in my own interests, or those of my personal and professional associates. One important aspect of the duty of loyalty is to retain the confidentiality of information that is explicitly deemed confidential by NAME OF ORGANIZATION, as well as information that appears to be confidential from its nature or matter. The duty of loyalty also encompasses a Board member's obligation to avoid conflicts of interest.

Duty of Obedience

As a Board member and representative of this Board, I agree to refrain from engaging in any acts that may compromise NAME OF

ORGANIZATION's charter and bylaws, that are against the law, or that are prohibited or beyond the scope of NAME OF ORGANIZATION's power.

Duty of Care

As a Board member and representative of this Board, I agree to demonstrate the level of attention required of a Board member in all matters related to NAME OF ORGANIZATION, i.e., the "duty to be informed." I understand that as a Board member, I have the responsibility to be informed about an issue before making a business decision relating to the issue. I will fulfill the duty of care if, prior to making a decision, I consider all material information reasonably available to me. To fulfill the duty of care, I will follow deliberate procedures and consult with appropriate committees, officers, and administrators of NAME OF ORGANIZATION as appropriate, or other outside experts in making corporate decisions. I understand that duty of care extends to the oversight of financial management obligations.

In addition, my signature below indicates my understanding of and willingness to comply with the following during my term(s) of service:

Orientation and the Basic Understanding of the Mission for New Members

I understand that in order to be an effective and productive Board member, it is my responsibility to have a thorough knowledge of NAME OF ORGANIZATION. By agreeing to serve on this Board, attendance at a formal orientation to NAME OF ORGANIZATION and Board membership is required prior to my first meeting.

Continuing Education

I understand that in order to be an effective and productive Board member, it is my responsibility to participate in board leadership continuing education provided by board development or leadership training programs with expertise in trustee education training. My certificates of attendance will be kept on file. I understand that continuing education may be provided at Board meetings and special sessions, such as retreats, and that I should also seek out additional opportunities as they arise. By agreeing to serve on this Board, I will participate fully in continuing education as requested and needed.

Board Meeting Attendance

I understand the expectation that all Board members will attend all Board meetings (highly preferably in person, but at times it may be telephonically) and to be an active participant. Additionally, it is my duty to fully understand and engage in the roles and responsibilities of this Board as a member. It is clear that I cannot miss more than the number of meetings stated in the by-laws each year, or I may automatically be removed from the Board.

Committee Meeting Attendance

I understand that because part of my role on this Board is to provide critical input and support through a participative committee structure, I am expected to attend all committee meetings upon which I serve (highly preferably in person, but at times it may be telephonically). Additionally, it is my duty to fully understand and engage in the activities and responsibilities of Committees as a member of this Board. I also understand and accept that my failure to be an active participant may result in my removal from the Board.

Communications

I understand the expectation that all Board members will be responsive to emails and voicemails in a timely manner.

Personal Giving

I understand that my personal giving sends an important message to the community of my belief in NAME OF ORGANIZATION as a worthy investment and that it demonstrates in a concrete manner my commitment to this organization. I will also open doors to affluence or influence for the CEO, Board members, or its Executive Director as often as possible or at a minimum as stated by the Governance Committee in order to develop the long-term relationships necessary to provide NAME OF ORGANIZATION with increased resources.

Ambassadorship and Advocacy

I understand that because Board members are among the most natural and primary ambassadors and advocates of the organization for which they serve, attendance at NAME OF ORGANIZATION and community events is an important articulation of those roles. As a member of this Board, I agree to annually attend at least as stated by the Governance Committee organizational functions per year and attend as many outside events as possible or a minimum of as stated by the Governance Committee to represent this organization in my community, business, and social activities. I will also serve as an advocate through an awareness of the legislative, ethical, cultural, and social issues that impact our mission. I will provide staff with a record of my attendance at such events.

Confidentiality

Access to information as required by law notwithstanding, I understand that Board members are often privy to information that is deemed confidential to protect the integrity of business planning and implementation. As a member of this Board, I understand that I am not an official spokesperson for the organization (unless specifically delegated by the Board), I will honor the confidentiality of information learned within the confines of Board or committee meetings, I will not distribute any organization documents other than public relations materials to anyone, and will return documents upon request. I will sign a confidentiality agreement annually signifying my understanding of and agreement with this condition and agree that my violation of the confidentiality of organizational documents or knowledge will result in my immediate removal from the Board.

Conflict of Interest

I agree to sign a conflict of interest statement annually. In addition, between the times that I sign the conflict of interest statement, I agree to notify NAME OF ORGANIZATION immediately should a real, potential, or perceived conflict of interest arise, as soon as it may arise.

Agreed this _____ day of ____, 20__ as a member of the NAME OF ORGANIZATION Board of Directors.

_____

Signature of Board Member:

_____

Name of Board Member (print)

_____

Signature of Governance Committee Chair

_____

Name of Governance Committee Chair (print)

Source: Katha Kissman.

Board Orientation

An emerging best practice is the formal orientation of the new members of the board:

- *To the organization:* its programs, history, pressing issues, finances, facilities, organization chart
- *To the board:* board member responsibilities, committee structure, bylaws, recent minutes, and list of board members

A good Board Leadership Manual for incoming board members is the strong foundation to a formal orientation process. The Manual should be comprehensive and contain the basic documents and most recent strategic plan, which are needed to fully acquaint and inform new board members of basic organizational information so that they can perform their fiduciary duties. It is recommended that the Board Leadership Manual also include:

- A copy of the organization's most recent IRS 990 filing
- The most recent audited financial statement
- Current and past year organizational budgets
- Copies of the past year board and committee meeting minutes
- Any other currently relevant documents
- All materials dated with revision dates
- Procedure for updating the board manual

It is also recommended that the organizations consider the development of a password-accessed board portal on its website. In this "board members only" section, all organizational documents (bylaws, meetings schedules, calendars of organizational events, can be posted (and easily updated by staff as necessary) via .pdf files.

In a flatter, more responsive organization, it is not just the CEO who needs feedback on how things are going and what needs fixing. An information system should be able to provide any decision makers, regardless of title, the right information at the right time. Executive

Information System (EIS) really means *"Everybody's Information System.* (Lynch and Cross 1995)

Such a board portal can include tabs covering such information as:

Home: Basic information—board and staff member contact information, e-mail links, calendar of future meetings and organizational events

Governance: Bylaws, articles of incorporation, conflict of interest policy, ethics policy, whistleblower policy, board terms, other policies and procedures, strategic plan, duties of directors

Financial: Financial statements, investment policies, current overview of investments, 990s

Meetings: All materials for upcoming meetings posted 10 business days in advance of the meeting

Committees: Committee charters, board member assignments, reports

Programs: Overview of programs, staff reports, brochures and public relations materials

It is also recommended that organizations provide incoming board members with a well-planned, in-person presentation by other board members and staff for formal orientation. BoardSource is seeing a trend from the informal to formal orientation and onboarding of new board members.

Working as a consultant and researcher with more than 70 not-for-profits, I have found that new board member orientation can strengthen efforts to recruit board members and keep current ones active. Individuals prefer joining a board that helps them understand the organization's mission and challenges. Orientation programs can help board members feel more confident about governing, more empowered to oversee the not-for-profit strategic direction. Responding to the interests of new board members increases their board participation, which in turn results in a more engaged board that is capable of accomplishing more for the organization. (Marabella 2009)

A formal orientation process not only cuts the learning curve down; it also helps to build relationships and a team sensibility, which is a desired aspect of any governing board. Formal orientation also helps to prevent inadvertent misunderstandings about organizational direction and may prevent troublesome behaviors from resulting.

The following board orientation chart, taken from the Board-Source publication *The Board Building Cycle*, provides an outline for a basic board orientation. It is strongly recommended that current board members be involved in this entire orientation process as a refresher and review. The information presented at the orientation should be honest and the presentations should not be overwhelming. The orientation should take place at the organization's headquarters and include key staff. The Governance Committee should follow up with new board members after the orientation to answer any lingering questions.

Board Orientation Chart

About the Organization		
Information	**Issues**	**Presentation Options**
Program	Offer new board members a feel for the work of the organization—what it does, whom it serves, what difference it makes—to get them emotionally and intellectually connected and motivated.	■ Tour of facilities ■ Observation of/participation in program activities ■ Presentation by client, member, or program participant ■ Video, slides, film presentation ■ Verbal presentations ■ Written materials
Finances	Help new board members become informed about where money comes from, how it is spent, and the state of the organization's financial health, including their role in fundraising.	■ Presentation by chief executive, chief financial officer, or treasurer ■ Background materials (most recent audit, budget, financials), graphically presented, if possible ■ Presentation of fundraising strategy
History	Provide sufficient knowledge about the past so that the present makes sense. Also, help new board members see their own participation as part of the organization's ongoing story.	■ Stories told by old-timers ■ Pictures ■ Written materials
Strategic direction	Present a framework for new members to participate effectively. Clarify mission, vision, organizational values, and goals that inform organizational actions.	■ Presentation/discussion by the chief executive or board chair ■ Copy of strategic plan (or other documents, especially mission statement, if no plan is available.)
Organizational structure	Help new board members understand who does what and lines of accountability.	■ Copy of the bylaws, IRS determination letter ■ Organizational chart ■ Introductions to key staff members

(*continued*)

(continued)

About the Organization		
Information	**Issues**	**Presentation Options**
Board roles	Ensure that new members understand the roles of the board.	■ Presentation/discussion, preferably with the whole board involved
Board member responsibilities	Ensure that new board members understand their own responsibilities as board members.	■ Presentation/discussion ■ Signed agreement (job description), including conflict of interest and ethics statements
Board operations	Help new board members understand how the board operates so that they may participate effectively.	■ Board manual ■ Board mentors ■ Committee charges and member lists ■ Meeting schedule
Board members	Facilitate new board member integration with other members.	■ List of board members and biographical data ■ Time set aside for social interaction
Skills	Instruct new members on how to read a financial statement.	■ Written materials ■ Presentation by the treasurer or finance committee

Note: Consider including current board members in the entire orientation process as a refresher and review. © 2000, Sandra R. Hughes, Berit M. Lakey, and Marla J. Bobowick, *The Board Building Cycle*.

Source: Reprinted with permission of BoardSource.

Board of Directors' Meeting Evaluation Form

The purpose of this form is to evaluate overall effectiveness of the meeting process. Please rank the following items on a scale of 1–5 where a "1" does not meet your expectations and a "5" exceeds your expectations. This examination will demonstrate where changes can be made to increase productivity.

	Exceeds Expectations		Meets Expectations	Below Expectations	
The agenda is clear and sensible, supported by the necessary documents, and circulated prior to the meeting.	5	4	3	2	1
The Board Packet was provided to all meeting participants in a timely manner.	5	4	3	2	1
All board members were present.	5	4	3	2	1
All board members were prepared to discuss materials sent in advance.	5	4	3	2	1
Reports were thorough, clear, and contained needed information.	5	4	3	2	1

(continued)

(continued)

	Exceeds Expectations		Meets Expectations	Below Expectations	
Discussions were on target.	5	4	3	2	1
Directors were prepared and involved.	5	4	3	2	1
We avoided getting into administrative/ management details.	5	4	3	2	1
Diverse opinions were expressed and issues were dealt with in a respectful manner.	5	4	3	2	1
The chair guided the meeting effectively and members participated responsibly.	5	4	3	2	1
Appropriate board and staff assignments were made; next steps were identified and responsibility assigned.	5	4	3	2	1
The board focused on issues of strategy and policy.	5	4	3	2	1
Objectives for the meeting were accomplished.	5	4	3	2	1

	Exceeds Expectations		Meets Expectations	Below Expectations	
The meeting began and ended on time.	5	4	3	2	1
The meeting room was conducive to work.	5	4	3	2	1
We enjoyed being together.	5	4	3	2	1

Please provide further feedback/suggestions here:

Source: Adapted from materials written by Lou Benson, PhD and BoardSource's *The Board Building Cycle.*

Resources

ASAE

ASAE University is a trusted source of vetted, essential information, containing programs in the functional areas of association management, as well as leadership and governance. ASAE University face-to-face programs, certificate programs, and online courses are designed for CEOs, senior and midlevel staff, and future leaders—offered at levels to match knowledge and experience and according to ASAE learning principles with specific content for varied needs, from skilled faculty and leading experts in association/nonprofit management. For more information: www.asaecenter.org/education.

ASAE's bookstore, offering published resources, is at www.asaecenter.org/bookstore, and many models and samples pertinent to association management, accessible by ASAE members, can be found by searching "models and samples" from ASAE's home page at www.asaecenter.org.

The ASAE Foundation is a source of ongoing research in the field, including the study behind this book: www.asaecenter.org/foundation.

BoardSource Learning Center and Store

BoardSource's Learning Center includes a bookstore, hundreds of downloadable resources, and a calendar of live and online training programs on how good governance can shape an organization's missions, finances, and strategic direction.

https://www.boardsource.org/eweb/dynamicpage.aspx?webcode =BDSOnlineStoreLanding

Policy Governance

Policy Governance® is an integrated set of concepts and principles that describes the job of any governing board. It outlines the manner in which boards can be successful in their servant-leadership role, as well as in their all-important relationship with management. Unlike most solutions to the challenge of board leadership, its approach to the design of the governance role is neither structural nor piecemeal, but is comprehensively theory based. The model covers all legitimate intentions of corporate governance codes (including Sarbanes-Oxley), but in a far more comprehensive, theory-based manner. There are no royalties or license fees for use of the model; it is free to all. Service-mark protection is intended only to preserve the complete accuracy of the model.

www.carvergovernance.com/train.htm

CompassPoint Workshops

CompassPoint believes that the people who work and volunteer in the nonprofit sector should be invested in and cultivated. In particular, organizations that invest in their leadership, management, and net-working capacity are more likely to sustain impact over time and successfully advance their mission. Through their workshop program they work with thousands of nonprofits to support their staff development and provide them with the knowledge and skills needed for success on topics from fundraising and financial management to business planning and board governance.

www.compasspoint.org/workshopspage

IFC Global Corporate Governance Forum

While tailored for corporate entities, this organization may be beneficial to nonprofit and association governing boards.

http://www.ifc.org/wps/wcm/connect/Topics_Ext_Content/ IFC_External_Corporate_Site/Corporate+Governance

Organizational Websites

ASAE—The Center for Association Leadership: www.asaecenter.org

Association Forum of Chicagoland: www.associationforum.org

Association of Governing Boards of Universities and Colleges: www
.agb.org/

BoardSource: www.boardsource.org

Case Western Reserve University Weatherhead School of Management: http://appreciativeinquiry.case.edu/

Council on Foundations: www.cof.org

Donors Forum of Chicago: www.donorsforum.org

The Ethics Resource Center: www.ethics.org

Independent Sector: www.independentsector.org

National Council of Nonprofit Associations: www.ncna.org

The National Human Services Assembly: www.nassembly.org/
nassembly

Society of Human Resources Management: www.shrm.org

Panel on the Nonprofit Sector "Principles of Good Governance and Ethical Practice": www.independentsector.org/principles_guide_ summary

Also see various individual states' nonprofit associations.

References

Andringa, Robert C., and Ted W. Engstrom. 2001. *Nonprofit Board Answer Book*. Washington, DC: BoardSource.

Argyris, Chris. 1993. *Knowledge for Action: A Guide to Overcoming Barriers to Organizational Change*. San Francisco: Jossey-Bass.

ASAE. 2006. *7 Measures of Success*. Washington, DC: ASAE: The Center for Association Leadership.

ASAE 2011. *Benchmarking in Association Management: Governance Policies and Procedures*. Washington, DC: ASAE: The Center for Association Leadership.

Balogun, Julia, and Veronica Hope Hailey, eds. 2008. *Exploring Strategic Change*. London: Pearson Education.

Beatty, Richard W., and David O. Ulrich. 1993. "Re-Energizing the Mature Organization." In *Managing Change: Cases and Concepts*, ed. Todd D. Jick. Boston: Irwin McGraw-Hill.

Blanchard, Kenneth, and Norman Vincent Peale. 1988. *The Power of Ethical Management*. New York: Ballantine Books.

Block, Peter. 2000. *Flawless Consulting: A Guide to Getting your Expertise Used*, 2nd ed. San Francisco: Jossey-Bass/Pfeiffer.

BoardSource. 2001. *The Board Development Planner: A Calendar of Nonprofit Board Initiatives*. Washington, DC: BoardSource.

BoardSource. 2005. *The Source: Twelve Principles of Governance That Power Exceptional Boards*. Washington, DC: BoardSource.

BoardSource. 2006. *The Sarbanes-Oxley Act and its Implications for Nonprofits.* Washington, DC: BoardSource (revised January 2006).

BoardSource. 2008. *Exceptional Board Practices: The Source in Action.* Washington, DC: BoardSource.

BoardSource. 2013. *BoardSource Nonprofit Governance Index—2012.* Washington, DC: BoardSource.

Bridgespan. 2011. *Strategies for Changing your Organization's Culture.* www .bridgespan.org/Publications-and-Tools/Leadership-Effectiveness/ Lead-and-Manage-Well/Strategies-for-Changing-Organizations- Culture.aspx#.VCbPBhZRzLR.

Brothers, John, and Anne Sherman. 2012. *Building Nonprofit Capacity: A Guide to Managing Change through Organizational Lifecycles.* San Francisco: Jossey-Bass.

Brown, William A. 2007. "Board Development Practices and Competent Board Members: Implications for Performance." *Nonprofit Management and Leadership* 17(3): 301–317.

Bryson, John. 2011. *Strategic Planning for Public and Nonprofit Organizations: A Guide to Strengthening and Sustaining Organizational Achievement,* 4th ed. San Francisco: Jossey-Bass.

Butler, Lawrence M. 2007. *The Nonprofit Dashboard: A Tool for Tracking Progress.* Washington, DC: BoardSource.

By, Rune Todnem. 2005. "Organisational Change Management: A Critical Review." *Journal of Change Management* 5(4): 369–380.

Carpenter, Brian L. 2007. *The Five Dysfunctions of Charter School Boards.* Mt. Pleasant, MI: National Charter Schools Institute. www .nationalcharterschools.org.

Carroll, John L. 2001. *Club Board Member's Guide: How to Become an Effective Member of your Club Board.* Sarasota, FL: Pineapple Press.

Carver, John. 2011. *Boards That Make a Difference: A New Design for Leadership in Nonprofit and Public Organizations,* 3rd ed. San Francisco: Jossey-Bass.

Chait, Richard P. 2003. *How to Help Your Board Govern More and Manage Less.* Washington, DC: BoardSource.

Chait, Richard P., William P. Ryan, and Barbara E. Taylor. 2005. *Governance as Leadership: Reframing the Work of Nonprofit Boards.* Washington, DC: Wiley/BoardSource.

Clemons, Calvin. 2011. *The Perfect Board*, 3rd ed. Baltimore, MD: Catharthis.

Coerver, Harrison, and Mary Byers. 2011. *Race for Relevance: Five Radical Changes for Associations.* Washington, DC: ASAE.

Collins, James Charles. 2001. *Good to Great: Why Some Companies Make the Leap—and Others Don't.* New York: Random House.

Compassion Capital Fund National Resource Center. 2014. *Working with Consultants.* Strengthening Nonprofits: A Capacity Builder's Resource Library. http://strengtheningnonprofits.org/resources/guidebooks/Working_with_Consultants.pdf.

Connolly, Paul M. 2006. *Navigating the Organizational Life Cycle: A Capacity Building Guide for Nonprofit Leaders.* Washington, DC: BoardSource.

Connor, Darryl R. 2006. *Managing at the Speed of Change*, 2nd ed. New York: Random House.

Cooperrider, David Loy. 1986. *Appreciative Inquiry: Toward a Methodology for Understanding and Enhancing Organizational Innovation* (PhD Dissertation). Cleveland, OH: Case Western Reserve University.

Cornforth, Chris. 2012. "Nonprofit Governance Research: Limitations of the Focus on Boards and Suggestions for New Directions." *Nonprofit and Voluntary Sector Quarterly* 41(6): 1116–1135.

Crutchfield, Leslie R., and Heather McLeod Grant. 2008. *Forces for Good: The Six Practices of High-Impact Nonprofits.* San Francisco: Jossey-Bass.

Cummings, Thomas G., and Christopher G. Worley. 2009. *Organization Development and Change.* Mason, OH: South-Western Cengage Learning.

Cummings, Thomas G., and Christopher G. Worley. 2015. *Organization Development and Change*, 10th ed. Stamford, CT: Cengage Learning.

Dietel, William M., and Linda R. Dietel. 2001. *The Board Chair Handbook*. Washington, DC: BoardSource.

Duhigg, Charles. 2012. *The Power of Habit: Why We Do What We Do in Life and Business*. New York: Random House.

Eadie, Douglas. 2004. *High-Impact Governing in a Nutshell: Seventeen Questions That Board Members and CEOs Frequently Ask*. Washington, DC: ASAE.

Eisenhardt, Kathleen M., and Melissa E. Graebner. 2007. "Theory Building from Cases: Opportunities and Challenges." *Academy of Management Journal* 50(1): 25–32.

Fisher, B. Aubrey. 1980. *Small Group Decision Making*. 2nd ed. New York: McGraw-Hill.

Gazley, Beth. 2014. "Good Governance Practices in Professional Associations for Public Employees: Evidence of a Public Service Ethos?" *Public Administration Review* 74(6): 747–759.

Gazley, Beth. 2015. "Governance: An Introduction." In: *ASAE Handbook of Professional Practices in Association Management*, 3rd ed., ed. John B. Cox. San Francisco: Jossey-Bass.

Gazley, Beth, and Ashley Bowers. 2013. *What Makes High Performing Boards: Effective Governance Practices in Member-Serving Organizations*. Washington, DC: ASAE Foundation.

Gladwell, Malcolm. 2000. *The Tipping Point: How Little Things Can Make a Big Difference*. New York: Little, Brown.

Glaser, Barney G., and Anselm L. Strauss. 2009. *The Discovery of Grounded Theory: Strategies for Qualitative Research*. New Brunswick, NJ: Transaction Publishers.

Grace, Kay Sprinkel. 2003. *The Nonprofit Board's Role in Setting and Advancing the Mission*. Washington, DC: BoardSource.

Guo, Chao. 2012. "The Road Less Traveled: Establishing the Link Between Nonprofit Governance and Democracy." December 31. *The Nonprofit Quarterly*. https://nonprofitquarterly.org/governancevoice/21562-the-road-less-traveled-establishing-the-link-between-nonprofit-governance-and-democracy.html.

Gupta, Babita, Lakshmi S. Iyer, and Jay E. Aronson. 2000. "Knowledge Management: Practices and Challenges." *Industrial Management and Data Systems* 100(1): 17–21.

Hammond, Sue Annis. 1996. *The Thin Book of Appreciative Inquiry*. Plano, TX: Thin Book Publishing.

Hammond, Sue Annis, and Cathy Royal, eds. 1998. *Lessons from the Field: Applying Appreciative Inquiry*. Plano, TX: Practical Press.

Harris, Margaret. 1993. "Exploring the Role of Boards Using Total Activities Analysis." *Nonprofit Management and Leadership* 3(3): 269–281.

Harrison, Yvonne D., and Vic Murray. 2014. "The Effect of an Online Self-Assessment Tool on Nonprofit Board Performance." *Nonprofit and Voluntary Sector Quarterly*. Published online before print November 25. doi: 10.1177/0899764014557361.

Heimovics, Richard D., and Robert D. Herman. 1990. "Responsibility for Critical Events in Nonprofit Organizations." *Nonprofit and Voluntary Sector Quarterly* 19(1): 59–72.

Herman, Robert D., and David O. Renz. 1999. "Theses on Nonprofit Organizational Effectiveness." *Nonprofit and Voluntary Sector Quarterly* 28(2): 107–126.

Holland, Thomas P., and David C. Hester. 2012. *Building Effective Boards for Religious Organizations: A Handbook for Trustees, Presidents, and Church Leaders*. San Francisco: Jossey-Bass.

Hughes, Sandra R., Berit M. Lakey, and Marla J. Bobowick. 2000. *The Board Building Cycle*. Washington, DC: BoardSource.

Huy, Quy Nguyen. 1999. "Emotional Capability, Emotional Intelligence, and Radical Change." *Academy of Management Review* 24 (2): 325–345.

Ingram, Richard T. 2003. *Ten Basic Responsibilities of Nonprofit Boards*. Washington, DC: BoardSource.

Isabella, Lynn. 1993. "Managing the Challenges of Trigger Events: The Mindsets Governing Adaptation to Change." In *Managing change: Cases and Concepts*, ed. Todd D. Jick. Boston: Irwin McGraw-Hill.

Jackson, Phil, and Hugh Delahanty. 2014. *Eleven Rings: The Soul of Success*. New York: Penguin.

Jäger, Urs Peter, and Florian Rehli. 2012. "Cooperative Power Relations between Nonprofit Board Chairs and Executive Directors." *Nonprofit Management and Leadership* 23(2): 219–236.

Jick, Todd D., ed. 1993. *Managing Change: Cases and Concepts.* Boston: Irwin McGraw-Hill.

Kaplan, Robert S. 2001. "Strategic Performance Measurement and Management in Nonprofit Organizations." *Nonprofit Management and Leadership* 11(3): 353–370.

Kissman, Katha. 2006. *Taming the Troublesome Board Member.* Washington, DC: BoardSource.

Kissman, Katha. 2009. *Trouble at the Top: The Nonprofit Board's Guide to Managing an Imperfect Chief Executive.* Washington, DC: BoardSource.

LaFasto, Frank, and Carl Larson. 2001. *When Teams Work Best.* Thousand Oaks, CA: Sage.

Lally, Phillippa, Cornelia H. M. Van Jaarsveld, Henry W. W. Potts, and Jane Wardle. 2010. "How are Habits Formed: Modelling Habit Formation in the Real World." *European Journal of Social Psychology* 40(6): 998–1006.

Lancaster, Lynne C., and David Stillman. 2002. *When Generations Collide: Who They Are, Why they Clash, How to Solve the Generational Puzzle at Work.* New York: HarperCollins.

LaPiana, David. 2000. *The Nonprofit Mergers Workbook: The Leader's Guide to Considering, Negotiating, and Executing a Merger.* Saint Paul, MN: Amherst H. Wilder Foundation.

LaPiana, David, Heather Gowdy, Lester Olmstead-Rose, and Brent Copen. 2012. *The Nonprofit Business Plan: The Leader's Guide to Creating a Successful Business Model.* New York: Turner.

Lieberman, David J. 2005. *How to Change Anybody.* New York: St. Martin's Press.

Lynch, Richard L., and Kelvin F. Cross. 1995. *Measure Up! How to Measure Corporate Performance.* New York: John Wiley & Sons.

Marabella, Santo D. 2009. "Tool 6: Reaping the Benefits of Improved Orientation." In *Getting on Board with Effective Orientation: A BoardSource Toolkit*, 16–17. Washington, DC: BoardSource.

Miller-Millesen, Judith L. 2003. "Understanding the Behavior of Nonprofit Boards of Directors: A Theory-Based Approach." *Nonprofit and Voluntary Sector Quarterly* 32(4): 521–547.

Moyers, Richard L. 2006. *The Nonprofit Chief Executive's Ten Basic Responsibilities*. Washington, DC: BoardSource.

Myatt, Mike. 2012. "How to Lead Change." *Forbes*, February 7. www.forbes.com/sites/mikemyatt/2012/02/07/how-to-lead-change-3-simple-steps/.

Nadler, David A., Beverly A. Behan, and Mark B. Nadler, eds. 2005. *Building Better Boards: A Blueprint for Effective Governance*. San Francisco: Jossey-Bass.

Ostrower, Francie. 2007. *Nonprofit Governance in the United States: Findings on Performance and Accountability from the First Representative Study*. Washington, DC: Urban Institute.

Preserving the Public Trust Initiative 2005. *Illinois Nonprofit Principles and Best Practices*. Chicago: Donors Forum.

Quy, Nguyen Huy. 1999. "Emotional Capability, Emotional Intelligence, and Radical Change." *Academy of Management Review* 24(2): 325–345.

Reid, Wendy, and Johanne Turbide. 2012. "Board/Staff Relationships in a Growth Crisis: Implications for Nonprofit Governance." *Nonprofit and Voluntary Sector Quarterly* 41(1): 82–99.

Ross, Bernard, and Clare Segal. 2002. *Breakthrough Thinking for Nonprofit Organizations: Creative Strategies for Extraordinary Results*. San Francisco: Jossey-Bass.

Schein, Edgar. 1998. *Process Consultation Revisited: Building the Helping Relationship*. Reading, MA: Addison-Wesley.

Schneier, Craig Eric, Craig J. Russell, Richard W. Beatty, and Lloyd S. Baird, eds. 1994. *The Training and Development Sourcebook*, 2nd ed. Amherst, MA: Human Resource Development Press.

Schwarz, Roger M., Anne S. Davidson, Margaret S. Carlson, and Susanne E. McKinney. 2005. *The Skilled Facilitator Fieldbook: Tips, Tools, and Tested Methods for Consultants, Facilitators, Managers, Trainers, and Coaches*. San Francisco: Jossey-Bass.

Seashore, Charles N., Edith Whitfield Seashore, and Gerald M. Weinberg. 1992. *What Did You Say? The Art of Giving and Receiving Feedback*, Columbia, MD: Bingham House.

Seem, Michael. 2001. *Leading Up: How to Lead Your Boss So You Both Win*. New York: Three Rivers Press.

Seligman, Martin E. P. 2002. *Authentic Happiness: Using the New Positive Psychology to Realize Your Potential for Lasting Fulfillment*. New York: Free Press.

Shani, Abraham B., and Gervase Bushe. 1987. "Visionary Action Research: A Consultation Process Perspective." *Consultation* 6 (Spring): 3–19.

Smith, Elizabeth A. 2001. "The Role of Tacit and Explicit Knowledge in the Workplace." MCB University Press. *Journal of Knowledge Management* 5(4): 311–321.

Solomon, Muriel. 1990. *Working with Difficult People*. London: Prentice-Hall International.

Stone, Melissa Middleton, and Francie Ostrower. 2007. "Acting in the Public Interest? Another Look at Research on Nonprofit Governance." *Nonprofit and Voluntary Sector Quarterly* 36(3): 416–438.

Susman, Gerald I., and Roger D. Evered 1978. "An Assessment of the Scientific Merit of Action Research." *Administrative Science Quarterly* 23(4): 582–603.

Tecker, Glenn H., Jean S. Frankel, and Paul D. Meyer. 2002. *The Will to Govern Well*. Washington, DC: ASAE: The Center for Association Leadership.

Trower, Cathy A. 2013. *The Practitioner's Guide to Governance as Leadership: Building High-Performing Nonprofit Boards*. San Francisco: Jossey-Bass.

Tuckman, Bruce W., and Mary Ann C. Jensen. 1977. "Stages of Small Group Development Revisited." *Group and Organizational Studies* 2(4): 419–427.

Tushman, Michael L., and Elaine Romanelli. 2009. "Organizational Evolution." In *Organization Change: A Comprehensive Reader*, eds.

W. Warner Burke, Dale G. Lake, and Jill Waymire S Paine. San Francisco: Jossey-Bass.

Useem, Michael. 2001. *Leading Up: How to Lead your Boss So You Both Win*. New York: Three Rivers Press. https://knowledge.wharton .upenn.edu/article/leading-up-the-art-of-managing-your-boss.

Watson, Thomas J. 1963. *A Business and Its Beliefs: The Ideas That Helped Build IBM*. New York, NY: McGraw-Hill.

Wertheimer, Mindy R. 2008. *The Board Chair Handbook*, 2nd ed. Washington, DC: BoardSource.

Weston, Marla, and Wylecia Harris. 2013. "A Century-Old Organization Faces Its Own Journey to the Next Century." *Nonprofit Quarterly* (Fall/Winter): 89.

Wheatley, Margaret J. 1992. *Leadership and the New Science: Learning about Organizations from an Orderly Universe*. San Francisco: Berrett-Koehler.

Wheelan, Susan A. 2005. *Creating Effective Teams: A Guide for Members and Leaders*, 2nd ed. Thousand Oaks, CA: Sage.

Wilcox, Jeffrey R. 2014. "The Changing Faces of Interim Executive Management: Strategic Capacity-Building for the Nonprofit Sector through Expert On-Demand Leadership." http://thirdsectorcompany .com.

Williams, Sherrill K., and Kathleen A. McGinnis. 2007. *Getting the Best from your Board: An Executive's Guide to a Successful Partnership*. Washington, DC: BoardSource.

Zemke, Ron, Claire Raines, and Bob Filipczak. 2000. *Generations at Work: Managing the Clash of Veterans, Boomers, Xers, and Nexters in Your Workplace*. New York: American Management Association.

About the Authors

Beth Gazley, Indiana University–Bloomington School of Public and Environmental Affairs, spent 16 years in the public and private sector workforce before pursuing a PhD. She currently teaches nonprofit management at undergraduate, graduate, and executive levels. Her scholarship addresses many aspects of public and nonprofit management capacity, intersectoral and interorganizational relations, and nonprofit public policy.

Gazley has collaborated with the ASAE: The Center for Association Leadership and the ASAE Foundation on three prior studies: *The Decision to Volunteer* (2008) and *The Decision to Give* (2010), both with Monica Dignam, and *What Makes High Performing Boards: Effective Governance Practices in Member-Serving Organizations* (2013, with Ashley Bowers). She also co-edited a special issue of *Nonprofit and Voluntary Sector Quarterly* on membership and mutual benefit associations, sponsored by the ASAE Foundation (2014, with Mary Tschirhart). Altogether Gazley has authored or co-authored more than 50 journal articles, op-eds, book chapters, reports, and other publications, many of which were written for practitioner audiences. Gazley is an active board member and has conducted workshops for numerous boards of directors. More at https://spea.indiana.edu/faculty-research/directory/index.html.

Katha Kissman is president and CEO of the Harbor Branch Oceanographic Institute Foundation. In addition, she is a BoardSource senior governance consultant as well as an independent nonprofit organizational development consultant.

As one of the nation's leading specialists in interim leadership, she has provided organizations with a short- or long-term leadership bridge and organizational development consulting. As an interim, she has handled turnarounds and organizations in crisis as well as those seeking strategic leadership to move to the next level of organizational growth. Her interim engagements have included the Association for Research on Nonprofit Organizations and Voluntary Action (ARNOVA), the National Flute Association, the Organization of American Historians, American Linguistic Society, the National Crime Prevention Council, and Hope For The Warriors. Previously, she served as national director, training and organizational development, for Volunteers of America, president and CEO of Leadership America, and managing director of the Round House Theatre. She was also on the founding teams of the American University of Sharjah in the United Arab Emirates and the American University of Kuwait.

Kissman is the author of BoardSource's *Taming the Troublesome Board Member* and *Trouble at the Top: The Nonprofit Board's Guide to Managing the Imperfect CEO*. She can be contacted at www.kathakissman.com.

Index